Introduction

I graduated from USC Dental School in 1949. I associated with another dentist in Culver City, California, for about a year and a half, and then was assigned to the United States Navy as a dental officer during the Korean War. After two years I returned to Culver City and opened my own practice.

The 1950s were the golden years for dentistry. There were few dental insurance companies, no HMOs, and no advertising. The only information I could put in the Yellow Pages was my name, phone number, and the fact that I was a member of the American Dental Association. My practice increased only by word of mouth. Patients were grateful and not demanding. Mothers stayed in the waiting room while I treated their children. Most kids were little heroes when they sat in the dental chair by themselves without doting mothers looking over my shoulder. I never "gassed" the kids with nitrous oxide gas or used general anesthesia when there were behavior problems. I would joke with the mothers saying, "I'll give you a prescription for elixir of phenobarbital, which is a mild sedative. Just give him/her a teaspoonful twenty minutes before the appointment, and you take three."

When I graduated from dental school, I knew how to make my own gold castings, build my own porcelain crowns, cast my own partial denture frameworks, weld the fixed bridges together, prepare teeth for crowns and bridges without a chair-side assistant, fabricate full dentures, and pour my own plaster models. Because of my excellent dental education, I knew precisely how all the mechanics of dentistry worked. Dentistry is a multifaceted profession, and in many cases an art form, which also requires extensive medical knowledge, mechanical expertise, manual dexterity, and a kind, gentle, chair-side approach to the patient. I always say, "The only time a dentist is a hero is when the patient has a toothache. Dentistry is an elective procedure except when the patient is in pain with a swollen jaw."

I worked standing up for more than thirty-six years. My patients sat in comfortable dental chairs, having their mouths rinsed out with water after each dental procedure, and being able to turn and spit into the cuspidor. Today, cuspidors have now for the most part been eliminated because of regulations that have been adopted that control their design. The "do-gooders" claimed that bacteria could be trapped in the flanges, and that spitting into a funnel attached to a suction tube was a more sterile and safe procedure. This tube/funnel set-up, along with laying the patients back in the chair, might be easier for the dentist, but it is miserable for the patients.

In contrast to the new, efficient, business-like offices, my practice was personal. My patients could always talk with me about their dental needs, their families, their hobbies, and their personal problems. They were all part of my dental family, and they always left the office happy with their treatment. I used gold and amalgam for most of my restorations except for the front teeth, which I restored with porcelain, gold foil, silicate cement, or three-quarter gold crowns. Dentists today don't use three-quarter crowns or gold foil because they are not taught such techniques.

A good three-quarter crown on an upper front tooth was a magnificent work of art that showed no gold from the front, but covered the back surface of the tooth in such a way as to impart strength and acceptable esthetics. Such restorations would last much longer than the insurance-mandated five years. Large insurance companies have for many years offered a dental option. The types of benefits are outlined in the Evidence of Benefits, which vary from plan to plan, but all have criteria that guide the dentist regarding the replacement of defective restorations. For example, crowns have been given an arbitrary lifetime of five years. Such limitations have carried over to the DHMO plans.

Not every patient wanted to hide the gold, however. One such patient was Mooey, our family nanny and cook (what desserts!), who was African-American. She had had a tiff with her husband in which he knocked out her front tooth. I wanted to place a fixed bridge with three-quarter crowns on the teeth on both sides of the space, then weld the porcelain-faced dummy tooth (pontic) to those crowns, and cement the units onto the supporting teeth (abutments). I told Mooey,

"By using these three-quarter gold crowns, I can conceal the metal in such a way that nobody would be able to tell that you have a fake tooth." "Oh no, Doctor," she said. "Show as much gold as possible! It would look great!"

This reminded me that many cultures have different concepts about good-looking dental esthetics. While teaching crown and bridge at USC dental school from 1949 to 1951, I saw many patients from other countries throughout the world. Many of these patients liked full gold crowns on their front teeth with precious stones set in them. I noticed when going to Mexico that many of the young people like stainless steel partial crowns on their front teeth. They also showed aluminum-colored frames around the front teeth.

A classmate of mine opened an office in Emeryville, California, home to large African-American and Hispanic populations in the 1950s. He specialized in pre-fabricated gold crowns for the front teeth that were fashioned from sheet gold and cost about $1 apiece. He would cut out the fronts of them leaving various shapes, like hearts, clubs, and diamonds. He charged $200 a crown, and his patients loved them.

Today, lip and tongue piercing, along with tattoos, are in vogue, replacing dental cosmetics. It's too bad. These procedures are a lot more expensive and much more deleterious and invasive than the gold veneers.

◆   ◆   ◆

When I finished work on a patient, I expected his dental restorations to last a lifetime No time limits were established to evaluate how long dental restorations would last, which unfortunately is the case nowadays with insurance companies. They use actuarial studies by non-dentists to arrive at covered benefits.

During the 1950s, dentists were held in high esteem, respected in the community, and were colleagues of their fellow practitioners.

When patients had a financial problem with their treatment, I would arrange a payment plan with the Bank of America. My office never had anything owing on the books. When patients are up-to-date on their bills, it's amazing how their fillings don't hurt, their dentures don't hurt, and the colors of the front crowns are just right.

Malpractice insurance was cheap because of the lack of plaintiff attorneys (a good thing). If some minor patient complaint arose, I could contact my insurance carrier over the phone without talking to a machine. The carrier would phone the patient and resolve the matter immediately. Contrast that with 1986, when my last patient was a seven-year-old. He climbed into the chair and said, "If you hurt me, I'll sue you." I kicked the little rascal out without even a look at the toy box.

The Beginning of the End

I could never figure out whose side the American Dental Association (ADA) was on. One of its big decisions marked the end of the respected dentist when it allowed dentists to advertise. Almost overnight the Yellow Pages were inundated with pictures of smiling patients, smiling dentists, and ridiculous claims. Advertising dental offices like Cowan, Painless Parker, Beauchamp, and Campbell had existed for many years, even though they were not sanctioned by the ADA. But they were licensed, and there was and still is no law forbidding advertising. Ad dental offices had never been recognized as a respectable part of the dental profession. Private practitioners considered the practice of advertising unethical.

Then the switch happened. Dentistry no longer was a respected ethical profession but a business where colleagues became competitors Dentists were now advertising not only in the Yellow Pages but also on radio and television. The dental profession was now competing on the same level as the disrespected ad offices .

Today, advertising fliers are left on your windshield, in your mailbox, and on your front porch. The ads are now on the Internet, on your fax machine, and your e-mail. Many dentists have Web sites showing a smiling dentist with happy, smiling children and adults, words of praise for his remarkably high standards, where he/she went to dental school, claims of reasonable fees, the insurances he takes, and guarantees that he uses the latest and best dental equipment. One mailer I received, a 3 x 8 inches card with a removable stub, stated that if I came into their dealership and test-drove a new BMW, I would get a "free" tooth bleaching by the advertising dentist, whose name and phone number were on the stub. Wow! Dentists are now in the same league as automobile salesmen.

I'm afraid that many patients today are being "suckered" by the market-happy dentist, who is dedicated to making money. Over-diagnosis of the need for dental treatment is prevalent in the profession. In later chapters I will demonstrate how dentists are taking advantage of uninformed patients. Just try to get your teeth cleaned and nothing else. It won't happen.

Loss of Independence

Things were great for the average ethical dentist in the 1950's. If the dentist diagnosed a procedure that was beyond his expertise, he would refer the patient to a specialist. The referred specialist, usually in those days was an oral surgeon. Most dentists did their own endodontics (root canals) and periodontics (gum health). I rarely referred to an oral surgeon because I did all my own oral surgery except when general anesthesia was required.

Early in my career, I had a new patient who was a skinny, bearded, and malnourished guy with a mouth that was an inflamed mess. He had a toothache, but there was so much infection in his mouth that I decided to refer him to an oral surgeon, who was my instructor in dental school and a renowned sexpot. The next morning, I got a phone call from him. He was furious. "Pedersen," he yowled, "that referral you sent me. The guy has syphilis! You son-of-a-bitch! If I get it this way, I'll never talk to you again." Maybe that's why I didn't refer much.

During my two-year stint in the navy, I was extracting as many as a hundred teeth a day in the boot camp dental clinic. We would line the patients (boots) up in a row of ten by the operating room door. They had already been diagnosed, and the teeth to be extracted were charted. I would inject the anesthetic in the first patient and have him go to the end of the line. By the time he got to the first spot, he was numb and ready for the extraction(s). This was an invaluable experience for me because I learned the latest techniques for all types of oral surgery, including setting fractures of the jaws.

Then it hit the fan.

A group of entrepreneurs came up with California Dental Practice Controls in the 1960s, which became Omega Dental. The idea was for Omega to arrange dental programs with insurance companies and sell plans to patients. They based their fees on a review of the fees submitted by dentists who signed with the program. Many of the dentists, including me, signed a contract with Omega. Omega sent out a form that contained most of the dental procedures with a place in which to write fees for particular procedures. I was advised by Omega to indicate fees for only the procedures that I performed, but I wrote fees for all the categories. This invited denials for payment. Dentists were paid by Omega when they mailed in the proper documentation noting the procedures that were performed. I was told that my fees for gold crowns ($60 in Culver City) were too high for the area. Beverly Hills dentists were entitled to higher fees because of their location. Thus, in their own way they contributed to price fixing. This plan was like a Preferred Provider (PPO) network, which is essentially the way most dentists operate today. When I received my monthly check from Omega, there would always be deductions for strange, obscure reasons. Then the usual phone call to Omega and the subsequent battle for pecuniary justice.

All the years I practiced, I worked mainly with Omega and as a PPO provider in addition to my private practice. Many patients began carrying dental insurance, which had exclusions and limitations and in most cases annual maximums. Patients usually struggled with their benefits. To this day, evidence of coverage (EOC) is still a mystery to most patients and is often misrepresented by dentists in order to maximize income.

The following is the story of my experiences in the dental HMO field, concluding with fictional short stories that summarize the "dental dilemma."

Chapter 1

The Beginning

I retired from active practice on December 1, 1986. I must say that to this day I miss my old patients and their families. In fact, I was a great-grand dentist. I had fun doing dentistry. Today I would not have fun doing dentistry; it would be a job, not a profession. Most dental practices now are large with many general dentists and specialists working on tight schedules. The cost to run these practices is enormous. All the dentists have to have chair-side assistants, business managers, and front desk people. Malpractice insurance, comprehensive medical coverage, and student loans place a heavy financial burden on the owner dentist. Being able to spend time with your patients and their families, watching their kids grow, hearing about the up-coming weddings, the graduations from high school, college, etc., and laughing and smiling, doesn't seem to happen today. It seems that it's all basically about money.

So it was in March of 1987 that I first heard about the Dental Health Maintenance Organization (DHMO). For the next twenty years, I worked for four different DHMO companies.

Any names mentioned in this book are not the actual names of the companies involved or the names of the people with whom I worked.

In March 1987, my son, Bob, told me about a DHMO that was in the process of selling its business to a group of investors. Bob was and still is in the industrial real estate business. One of the principals in the selling company was a business acquaintance of Bob's, who had been talking to the CEO of the selling company regarding vacating their offices, which they were renting through Bob's firm. He suggested that I talk to the CEO who was working with a dentist who represented a group that was going to buy the company.

So the CEO introduced me to Anthony Amato, D.D.S., who was one of the men investing in the company, which was to be named Den-Cap (DC). Dr. Amato was going to be the CEO of the newly formed company. We instantly became good friends. Everyone knew him as Tony. He was the best salesman I'd ever seen. He should have been pitching patent medicine off the back of a horse-drawn surrey. His enthusiasm was infectious. Tony explained how "capitation" works, the Knox-Keene laws of California, the need for a quality management committee, and the managing of the provider dentists. He said that he would know by May or June if he had control of the company, and when he gained control, he would hire me immediately to start the quality assurance program for the company.

Most competing DHMO systems are very similar, and the competition is fierce. The marketing people go out into the commercial field and speak to the human resources department (HR) of a certain company. Once the various types of dental programs are <u>accepted and rates established, an open enrollment takes place. At this time the benefits and options</u> are explained to the enrollees This sets the tone of the quality assurance business. Most people never read the directions for anything. (How many times have you read your auto owner's manual? Ever?) Most enrollees go home with the idea that everything is free. The evil exclusions and limitations of the programs usually do not sink in. Thus, when they go to see a DC provider, they expect everything to be free. Up pops the supercilious office manager, who tries to explain what is a benefit and what is an optional treatment, which are billed at the dentist's usual customary fees. This makes the dentist the bad guy. Situations like this often lead to grievances.

Every company has a provider relations department that handles the provider dentists and their complaints, which are usually about compensation and the eligibility lists of patients.

The dentists' compensation is in the form of a capitation (per head). They are paid so much per month per enrolled patient, whether he or she makes an appointment or not. Most dental procedures also have patient co-payments. The dentist makes his money from the co-payments of the patient and the monthly capitation. The idea is to give the provider dentist a monthly list of eligible patients and pay him or her the monthly capitation rate. The number of patients accessing the office is the utilization for that office. An office that is underutilized makes a lot of capitation money, but the office that has a high utilization rate can lose money because the operating expenses will exceed the income from the payments of capitation and the patient co-payments. This system seems to work if the company can maintain and add to its line of business. When a business drops its contract with the DHMO, the provider dentist must start over again with a new list of patients, taking the initial financial hit before getting the patient into a maintenance position (all extensive work completed and the patient placed on recall). It is imperative that the DHMO retain its existing book of business while acquiring new groups and individuals; otherwise, the dentist takes it in the shorts.

This is what makes the DHMO unique. The provider dentist assumes all the risk. Hence, the DHMO is not an insurance company but is strictly a benefits' company. The schedules of benefits (SOB) are established by competition with other similar companies. These schedules list a series of dental procedures with notations indicating co-payments, if any. For example, x-rays and exams often have a "0" co-pay, while the co-pay for a porcelain-fused-to-metal crown (PFM) might be $100 plus an additional charge for a noble metal instead of the covered "base" metal. (Most dentists claim that base metal is too hard and unworkable, while noble metals are softer and easier to fit to the prepared tooth.)

One interesting aspect about these plans is that a dentist is rarely or never consulted before the company's final printing of a SOB. I wasn't. Lay employees confer to create these benefits by comparing them to those of the competitors. Many SOBs list procedures that are never done or are obsolete. Therefore, you, the patient, should always read your benefits and be dental savvy before you meet the employee with the clipboard.

The schism between the business end of the company and the quality side has always existed since the creation of the DHMO. Quality Management (QM), which is necessary in California in order to comply with the Knox-Keene law, is basically the non-productive enemy of a profit-making enterprise. QM is the same thing as QA, quality assurance, a title that is not being used currently.

However, QM does set the tone for the efficient and ethical delivery of dental services. According to most surveys conducted by the DHMOs, more than 80 percent of their patients are happy with their treatment and continue their recalls with those dentists. One major advantage with a capitation plan is that for dentists who have a small patient list and/or are just starting out, the DHMO provides an immediate source of patients. As Tony said, "An empty chair produces nothing." It is not a bad idea for the young dentist just starting out to sign up with the DHMOs to fill those empty chairs.

Tony lived up to his word, and in May 1987 I started working for a DHMO. The company already had a provider list of participating dentists, mostly in San Bernardino County, Riverside County, and Los Angeles County. The company had a CEO, many stockholders, a Knox-Keene license, and an office in a new ten-story Orange County office building. It had a marketing department, computer department, provider relations, grievances, billing and claims, and all the other departments necessary to the success of a DHMO. I invested in the company, along with at least six other investors.

Chapter 2

The First Challenge

My first job for someone other than myself was to set up a program for Quality Management (QM), a necessity under Knox-Keene. I would go out to the various general dentists who were on the company's roster and evaluate their facilities and their chart documentation to ensure that they were in compliance with the quality standards established by the law. Our company was under the watchful eye of the California Department of Corporations (DOC), which administered the Knox-Keene criteria and would perform periodic audits of our company, both fiscally and quality-wise. The DOC also would check to see how QM handled grievances from the patients and the thoroughness of our audits.

In order to perform the required audits, some type of standardized form was going to be needed that would enable an evaluation of the facility itself and an evaluation of the patient files. But, at the beginning, I rated the offices on a scale of one to ten, ten being the highest. When I returned to corporate, I would complete my evaluation, adding comments and grades from one to ten. The grades were then put into the computer system, which also contained all the appropriate credentialing of the participating dentists. Provider Relations (which was also me) kept the files on all of the provider dentists. The customer service representative would call and ask about the quality of a certain dentist. I would recommend the provider with the highest number first if the facility were conveniently located. Lower scorers were recommended next with location being an important issue for the patient. Only offices that had scores above six were referred. Offices that scored below six were appointed for re-auditing and closed to new patients until they had a passing score.

Then I was introduced to one of the first shareholders of DC, an oral surgeon, Dr. John Schnell, from northern California. Tony wanted me to work with John to create an auditing tool that would produce a scoring percentage. The score would evaluate both the physical quality of the facility and the accuracy of its charting and diagnoses. The score would indicate when the office should be re-audited.

John and I went together to review an office and see if our form made sense. John was incredible. He was the most relaxed man I'd ever met. He would sleep while I drove to our appointed facility. The practice we visited was in the poorer part of town and housed in an antiquated building. We brought with us a notebook outlining the regulations the state had created and expected us to adhere to and enforce established criteria. It was a shock to us, and especially me, to see a facility with a business office occupied by an army of people who ignored the piles of records scattered about the room, the absolute chaos of a full waiting room, and very few English-speaking people jammed into worn, plastic-covered chairs. The office had ten operating rooms, a lab, a darkroom, two restrooms, and a large lunchroom.

We plowed through the clutter to a small room where we were seated and allowed to peruse the thick records, which contained bare-minimum x-rays and writing in the documentation that was for the most part illegible. As I said to John, "Such writing would make my personal physician feel vindicated for his lousy scribbles."

The office flunked the audit. However, the owner/doctor was very pleasant, mainly because our approach to the audit was not the least bit punitive in nature. We collected copies of the participating dentists' licenses, their evidence of malpractice insurance, their DEA (prescription drugs and narcotics) licenses, and a copy of their diplomas. After almost four hours, the review was complete, with the doctor signing off and agreeing to have a six-month re-audit.

Completed audits were entered into the computer system, which would set a date for the next audit of that facility. When an office scored low, the company would have the peer committee (made up of select provider dentists, Tony, and me) review that office in order to determine whether it should be terminated from its contract with DC. Terminating an office for quality was a difficult process involving the State Board of Dentistry and the DOC. Normally a poor performer could be terminated for failure to comply with the provider contract.

One of the office personnel, Betty, was designated to help me with the scheduling of offices to be reviewed. She would call the offices and assign my appointments for me. One time she sent me to Banning, California, for a 9:00 AM appointment. I knocked on the door to what appeared be a dental office even though there was no sign. When the door opened, I soon realized I had been appointed to audit a whorehouse! That incident has been rehashed through the years, with lots of smart remarks from my colleagues. They were either skeptical or jealous.

Another memorable encounter with a new provider review occurred in Hemet. I drove there to audit the office of Dr. Jerome O'Kelly, who I assumed was an Irishman. When I got there, I found an office in a single house that appeared to have been built in the 1920s. It had a front porch and heavy, partial glass front door. I went into the large waiting room, which was the former living room of this old house. There was nobody in sight. I looked around the room, which was carpeted with ugly "high-low" deep pile carpeting. The room was lined with folding chairs except for one area near the former fireplace. There stood a large aviary with all sorts of birds and parrots squawking and tweeting. The room stunk so bad that I gagged.

I looked around and saw a little homemade alcove with a countertop; I saw no one. Then I heard a high-pitched voice from behind the counter. I looked over the top of the counter and saw a very small, dark-skinned lady. She asked, "What do you want?"

I said, "I'm Dr. Pedersen from Den-Cap, and I have an appointment with Dr. O'Kelly to review his office to see if it is up to state standards in order for him to continue as a provider."

Just then in walks Dr. O'Kelly, a very short Hindu dentist with a high-pitched voice. He was definitely not an Irishman. He walked me through the office, showing me his two dingy operating rooms and a cluttered, filthy lab. Then in another larger room, he showed me several up-right pianos in various stages of repair. This was his hobby, and he was very proud of the pianos. He never once talked about dentistry. I'm thinking, *Where am I? Am I crazy? What is this?*

Then Jerome said, "I have been receiving many Den-Cap patients, but after I examine them, they don't come back." No kidding! This was my only experience with an Irish-named Hindu dentist in a smelly bird guano laced, filthy dental office. Needless to say, he was terminated from the plan. How he got on the plan in the first place is still a mystery. The only possible explanation is that the former DHMO was desperate for provider dentists and accepted any office without having a provider-relations representative at least look at the office.

When brokers and agents work to sell the DHMO plans, the Human Resources (HR) people look for two things: benefits and the number of providers. The longer the list of providers, the better the impression on the HR person. That's why many plans sign on dentists without performing thorough office reviews. When a bad dentist signs on as a provider, it is incumbent on the patient to immediately call the plan and change providers.

Chapter 3

Learning Humility

After the incident with the whorehouse in Banning, I did my own scheduling of panel providers. I made the necessary phone calls, schmoozing the office managers and establishing a good rapport with the staff. The auditing was going well in the quest for timely compliance with the DOC requirements. I was feeling pretty good about myself.

Then the need for audits waned for a while. So early in my career with DC, Tony decided the company should have a presence in northern California. At this time, the company had providers in the counties of San Bernardino, Riverside, Los Angeles, San Diego, Kern, Fresno, and Ventura. DC was not a big player in northern California. Thus, I became a recruiter and embarked on a recruiting tour of northern California, hoping to increase the provider panel.

DC had a small marketing office located in Walnut Creek. One of my arrangements with Tony was that I could on most occasions have my wife, Gloria, come along with me on the trips, which made it much more pleasant for both of us. The company did not expense my wife, so I was very careful watching expenses, never taking advantage of the company.

In Walnut Creek I met with two women in the marketing office. One, Georgia, was essentially a secretary for Tony, handling the few small contracts they had. The other, Lois, handled marketing. Lois had been in the marketing business of medical HMOs and dental HMOs for many years. She lived in Danville, which is south of Walnut Creek and in many respects is the elitist corner of the East Bay—beautiful estates surrounded by an expensive private country club. Georgia and Lois were very helpful and patient.

Gloria and I had dinner with Lois and her husband at a quaint Italian restaurant in Danville. We then retired to their sumptuous home for after-dinner coffee and talk. Lois taught me a lot about the relationships between marketing agents and insurance brokers. I hadn't realized that brokers even existed, and that they were the actual go-betweens for the HMOs and the HR personnel of the potential buyers of the plans. All the companies dealt with such brokers, who then assisted in the marketing of their products.

The major references I used to start my recruiting endeavors were the Yellow Pages and the Thomas Guide. I set aside my anti-advertising biases and quickly became engulfed in finding prospects for DC. I carried the company brochures and a laptop presentation in preparation for interviews with prospects. I became a team player, and as I gradually learned the mechanisms of HMOs, I became an advocate for them.

The main thing I did when talking to doctors was to tell the truth, explaining how DC did business, how it planned to treat the doctors, how it got enrollees, and how many patients they could expect to have assigned to them. I told them that since DC is in the building phase, it might take some time before they see significant additions to their clientele. I also told them that at any time if they were dissatisfied, they were under no obligation to continue with DC.

This technique is contrary to most marketing approaches. I don't mean to imply that marketing people fail to tell the truth, but they do tend to exaggerate, leaving many important issues unaddressed.

My task was formidable, since northern California dentists harbored a deep hatred for capitation plans. This was a period in my new dental life where I learned humility and how to not take rejection personally. Many dentists and office managers doubted my family lineage. The biggest challenge was attempting to talk to any of the doctors by getting past the front desk. Those front desk women were very tough and very protective of their doctors, often resembling a lioness with her cubs.

My first big accomplishment was finding a dental center in Walnut Creek where the front desk people treated me like a human being. I spent a long time with the pleasant office manager, explaining the benefits of contracting with DC. This office had everything: general dentists and specialists, just what Tony needed. That afternoon I called him with the good news and explained that all I had to do was to see the office again in the morning, and they would have the signed contracts and appropriate documentation ready. Then Tony asked me their name and I said, "SmileTech & Vision." He hit the ceiling!

"You big dope," Tony said, "you're signing with one of our biggest competitors!" (Fifteen years later, I would go to work for them.)

I was in the middle of a great dental dilemma, but undeterred and determined.

The trip turned out to be a muted success, because I contracted several good offices throughout the East Bay area. I found an office in Pleasanton, one in Concord, one in Martinez, and one in San Ramon. These cities were within a twenty-mile radius of Walnut Creek.

John, my oral surgeon friend from the company, had his office in Fairfield, which is just across Suisun Bay from Walnut Creek and Concord. Since we were so close, Gloria and I decided to meet John and his wife, Pat, for dinner. This gave me a chance to review what I had accomplished with him. We both agreed that it appeared that DC was on its way to becoming a factor in the DHMO business. After dinner we went to their home in the hills northwest of Fairfield. It was a very attractive, rustic place, which Pat contended was haunted. She showed us the room where strange sounds have been heard. We sat there for several minutes, poised to hear ghostly noises, but nothing ever manifested. It was possible that this might have been a leg-pulling encounter. John never owned up.

The four of us became close friends, and when we were in the area, we would always get together and take side trips around the North Bay area, especially enjoying Sausalito and Tiburon. The many antique shops and quaint restaurants in a spectacular setting offer a wonderful view of the bay and the San Francisco skyline.

Chapter 4

My First Cell Phone

I had been traveling all over California performing audits of existing panel providers and recruiting. In 1989 Tony broke down and let me have a cell phone. I had been communicating with the main office and making appointments for audits using phones at 7-Eleven stores. I think I have used the phone in all the 7-Eleven stores in California. These convenience stores were also my main source of lunch.

My new cell phone was an early Motorola model. Even though it was huge and looked like a small portable radio with a large antenna, it was a bonanza for me. When I went to the Santa Rosa area to recruit with my new phone, I had a newly hired dental consultant with me, Dr. Dave Monroe, who was training to be an auditor for DC. We both were in awe of the new creation. But after several months of using the device, Tony called me and screamed at me about the excessive charges for the phone. Providers had my cell phone number, and when questions arose they would call me, and I obliged them by having lengthy conversations. So I was ordered to return to the 7-Elevens.

Dave was phasing out his practice in Sacramento, and he was a great help to me in signing new offices in some of the hard Sacramento areas. When Dave was in Orange County, he would stay over at a hotel near the main office. He was with me on the way to having dinner at my home when the San Francisco earthquake hit. We were listening to the World Series on the car radio when it hit. The radio description was wild. One of my colleagues was almost killed when the Oakland part of the Bay Bridge collapsed as he was leaving his office.

Dave became a close friend who would always have dinner with me in Sacramento when I was up there. Sadly, Dave had a stroke and lost the use of his right side as well as a good deal of his speech. It happened after he learned that his wife of forty years had decided to leave him because she wanted her space. (That seems to be the norm nowadays.) After a short time Dave passed away.

Dave had introduced me to Dr. Sean O'Reilly, an older dentist who had practiced many years in the Fair Oaks area of Sacramento. He was a large, ruddy man who liked his spirits. He had a strange office that was in a rustic building with a floor plan similar to a fun house. He no longer practiced himself, but still wanted to contract with DC. The only dentist in the office had suspect abilities.

I did my best to straighten the place out, but we could never get it up to an acceptable standard that would enable them to sign a contract. In spite of this, Sean was a big help to me, since he had been active in the local politics as well as in the Dental Society. His expertise would come in handy later on.

Chapter 5

Dog and Pony Shows

Tony was a firm believer in the persuasive benefits for provider recruitment that are derived from entertaining the potential providers. He called these "dog and pony shows," and he plied the new doctors and their staffs with good food and drink prior to delivering his pitch extolling the benefits of becoming a DC provider. Tony tended to quote numbers and percentages, and I constantly reminded him to refrain from doing so, because the numbers were not accurate or just plain not true. Yet, there is no question that they were successful. DC continued to expand because he presented these shows all over the state. Even the number of new providers in the northern part of the state was growing, especially after his sessions of elegant wining and dining.

About this time, Tony hired another dental consultant, Dr. Peter Paulsen, who helped with the audits and performed other supportive jobs for DC.

There was one instance where the show almost failed, but as usual, Tony landed on his feet. DC was in the process of receiving a contract with a senior citizens group in Hemet, which has a large senior population loaded with widows and retirees. My job was to go to Hemet and find providers who would sign with DC and serve the senior group. I worked hard and long and lined up a potential list of thirteen offices. It was only a question then of getting the contracts signed. I told Tony about this, and, of course, he immediately came up with the idea of a dog and pony show in Hemet entertaining the prospects and explaining how the plans work. So I made the plans for a catered dinner at the Holiday Inn and invited the prospects and their staffs. All responded and agreed to the time and the place. Tony arranged for Italian-style meals and the wine.

Tony, Betty, Peter and I all arrived at the Holiday Inn in Hemet about an hour ahead of time in order to set up the tables and make arrangements with the caterer. Tony brought several cases of Italian Chianti along to go with the meal. Peter, Betty and I set up the tables with red-checkered tablecloths and red napkins while Tony opened up twelve bottles of Chianti and set them on the tables. It looked great. There were also candles, four to a table, and piped-in Italian music.

The dentists and their staffs arrived virtually at the same time and very punctually. They all looked in awe at the table settings and the uncorked Chianti bottles. But they were all teetotalers. Yikes!

Peter and I proceeded to get soft drinks out of the hotel vending machines as quickly as possible. Of course, the machines contained only a few cans (it had been a hot day; in fact, most of the days in Hemet are too hot), so on we went to the local stores. We finally succeeded in getting enough sodas and waters to satisfy the group.

The dinner of lasagna, meatballs, and spaghetti was fantastic. Tony got up and delivered his pitch and, as usual, handled the group with an enthusiastic talk and excellent responses to the questions. The result was that twelve of the thirteen offices signed up that night. The dental program for the seniors was a serious success and marked a significant beginning of growth for DC.

◆　　◆　　◆

One dentist in San Jacinto, which is next to Hemet, brought up an interesting issue. He was a hyper guy who was in the process of a divorce and living in a trailer in back of his office, which was a one-story house-like structure. He refused to sign up with us unless we would allow him to use only composite filling materials and no silver amalgam. Silver amalgam does contain some mercury, but the amount in a filling has been shown to be insignificant as far as toxicity is concerned. (The American Dental Association has gone on record supporting the use of amalgam. Trillions of amalgams are in the mouths of millions of people, and reports of toxicity are rare.)

I asked him why he was so adamant about not using amalgam. He told me, "I had this ten-year-old female patient who needed four small fillings on her four six-year molars. I placed small amalgam restorations in those teeth. About a year later, the mother came into my office in tears. Her daughter was in a multiple sclerotic-like state, and her physicians were baffled. They suggested that the amalgam fillings be removed as a last resort. I removed the amalgam, placed temporary cements, and waited. She immediately got better, with all symptoms gone. I subsequently placed composite restorations, which were tolerated by the patient. I'm sorry, but I just can't bring myself to use amalgam anymore."

I had him sign the contract with the "no amalgam" stipulation. However, the debate still goes on in the profession. Most dentists are going toward the use of composite restorations not only for their apparent safety, but also because they are tooth-colored. Composite restorations at the present time are not as durable as amalgam and are not as dimensionally stable. The binders that are light-cured and cause adhesion of the filling to the tooth often cause sensitivity. This usually goes away after a while, but if it continues over a long period of time, the offending restoration should be replaced.

Chapter 6

The Growth

Using the home office phone, I worked hard to recruit offices in the Central Valley. It was not easy because most dentists didn't need the extra patients. Happily, I found one in Livingston, had several phone contacts with the dentist, and closed the deal. All that remained was to fax him a contract signed by Tony and have him sign and complete it. A few hours later, I received a call from the Livingston dentist. He asked me if Tony was the dentist who owned land in the Central Valley, whose wife's family owned vineyards, and had had a large practice in Gilroy. I said yes, which resulted in a tirade on what a "blankety-blank" Tony was, that he stole a lot of his land, and that he would not sign with anyone of his ilk.

I hadn't dug into Tony's background because I felt that the past was not an issue. I was very naïve, but that episode triggered my search into his past. He had owned two large practices in central California specializing in Medi-Cal patients. He also lectured at USC, often extolling the benefits of large practices with large Medi-Cal patient loads, as well as the developing DHMOs. However, the State Dental Board had revoked his license twice for improprieties in billing the state. But Tony always bounced back, and now he was the CEO of DC witnessing its phenomenal growth.

Tony was a Roman Catholic who went to 6:30 AM mass every morning before coming to the office. Usually, if Peter, who was very religious, were present, Tony would have him say a morning blessing. This was interesting because Tony's language was atrocious, and he engaged in a lot of "touchy-feely" behavior with the female staff members. He always bragged about his large family and their unabashed loyalty to him as the head of the household. At the end of a typical working day, I would remind him to be sure to go to mass the next morning to get his quick fix so he would be able to function all day long in a "forgiven" state.

Occasionally, a dentist who lived near Palm Springs and who represented the company in Riverside and San Bernardino counties visited Tony in the home office. This man, Dr. Gerald Horne, was the only person who generated fear in Tony, probably because he had such strong ties to the school boards and the teachers' unions in those counties, and thus generated considerable income for the company. He always fascinated me because he was a tall man who had a large, protruding growth in the middle of his forehead between his eyes. I laughed to myself because when talking with him my eyes always crossed. Then one day I was driving to Victorville to recruit providers. A pebble thrown from the wheel of a truck hit my new station wagon. The dent was a spot directly between the headlights, and you can guess who this reminded me of.

Gerald lived in Desert Hot Springs, a small community nestled in the hills north of Palm Springs. Toward the end of my career with DC, I ran into Gerald, who was a changed man. His demeanor had always been somewhat dour, but now he was different. He was smiling, happy, and exuberant. Then I noticed: the growth was gone! He had it surgically removed, had gotten a divorce, and bought a new, red Chevy convertible. He had retired and had a girlfriend. I never saw him again.

Chapter 7

Committees

Peer Review Committee

Each DHMO has a Peer Review Committee, which is a mandatory part of the policies and procedures manuals that are submitted to the DOC for approval. DC's Peer Review Committee met quarterly. The committee consisted of Tony, Gerald, me, and two other dentists from the Inland Empire, who were original shareholders in DC before it was called DC. Those two shareholders had huge enrollments from DC, and both saw an astounding number of DHMO patients per day.

Each meeting had an agenda, which usually reviewed specific grievances that involved quality of care. Usually a few cases were presented to the committee for its review and analysis. If the introduced documentation and radiographs indicated poor treatment by the dentist, unless extreme, the patient was reimbursed for any payments made toward the treatment, the charges were deducted from the dentist's monthly capitation check, and the patient was moved to another provider. In those extreme cases, the provider was immediately placed on "reserve." This means that the provider was not assigned any more new patients. The length of time on "reserve" depends on the seriousness of the deficiencies.

Any offending providers were contacted prior to the Peer Review Committee meeting and notified that they were welcome to come before the committee for appeal and present the case from their perspective.

Public Policy Meetings

Betty and I ran the Public Policy meetings, which were usually luncheons held in a restaurant in Riverside or San Bernardino counties. The invited attendees were representatives of the companies whose employees and their families were enrolled with DC. It was kind of a miniature dog and pony show. Gerald showed up at these lunches on occasion, which helped me because he schmoozed well and had a thorough knowledge of the plans and their exclusions and limitations. He also had a lot of authority and could create new deals or compromises on the spot.

These meetings always had a very positive effect, and Tony never complained about the costs. It seems that all CEOs are genetically averse to spending money, since all corporations employ "bean counters". However, the positive reactions to these get-togethers from the company reps and HR people justified such public relations endeavors. It was simply good business.

Grievances

I chaired the Grievance Committee, which met weekly. Grievances came from many sources, such as enrollees, providers, claims denials, and denied specialty referrals. The underlying theme of these meetings was "save money!" I confronted Tony with a complaint from one of the providers in San Bernardino, which was about the low co-payments for crowns, usually $50. The lab cost for such crowns was more than this, so how was the dentist supposed to pay his expenses?

Tony reflected on this problem and said, "We'll pay the provider $50 toward the lab charge, and $90 toward the charge for a removable prosthetic [partial denture and full denture], but don't tell any of the others!"

I said, "Are you crazy? If we pay one provider those benefits, the word will circulate to the others in a minute! We'll look like crooks playing favorites."

Thus, all providers received lab reimbursements for crowns and dentures. This deflected any impressions they might have that they were getting screwed.

The Grievance Committee usually reviewed only those complaints that involved the question of the quality of the dentistry performed. Most quality complaints came after the patients found out that their treatment was not completely covered and they had incurred legitimate co-payments. They should have read the fine print—same old story.

Chapter 8

The Department of Corporations

The Department of Corporations (DOC) performed random audits of all the functions of the company. The DOC would make an appointment to come and review the company, usually for a period of about four days. It would review all phases of the operations. This was panic time for Tony, and everyone in every department was jumping to be sure all documentation and procedures were in place.

The Quality Management (QM) department was in the DOC's crosshairs. Three or four dental consultants hired by the DOC were in charge of the reviews. They would earmark certain providers for audit, and it was my job to be sure they passed. It was all last-minute stuff.

For example, I was in Victorville doing a review of a dental provider when I received a call from Tony. He was very excited because the DOC had decided at the last minute to review a panel office in San Bernardino the next morning. I had never been to that facility. Tony said, "Ray, you're going to have to get your ass over there this afternoon. The DOC is sending three auditors to review them. You need to be sure that the place is clean and that they have satisfactory charting. They're tough and are going to be there the first thing tomorrow morning!"

So I headed for San Bernardino. I arrived there just after the lunch hour. The office was in a three-story, Spanish-style building of 1929 vintage. There were the usual thick stucco walls, the red tile roof, and the large, heavy wood doors. But inside, the office had the appearance of the Alamo. It was a dark and dingy dump. There was no waiting room on the first floor, which housed what appeared to be an attempt at an orthodontic office. The main office was on the second floor. There also was a large business office that was a mishmash of partially opened cardboard boxes with patient files lying on chipped Formica countertops. I saw several female assistants whose dress was somewhat short of professional, but I saw no doctor. Plaster and impression material were on the hallway walls. It looked as if the staff had thrown the stuff at each other.

I called all the people together and explained what was to happen the next morning. I told them to get the place cleaned up immediately. I showed them how to clean their business office and the lab, straighten out the operating rooms (which had old, poorly maintained equipment), and wash the hallway walls. I then went to the third floor, which housed a mass of storage files, and most likely would not be examined by the consultants. Thank god, because it was a filthy mess covered with Dracula-like cobwebs.

I finally met with the owner-dentist, who was back from lunch. I knew him from earlier years when he almost bought my practice. He was an interesting guy mainly because of his attitude toward dentistry. He would say, "I never want to get involved with the patient to the extent of knowing about their family, their hobbies, etc. I only want to do the diagnosis and turn the rest over to the staff. For example, if I need to make a crown on a molar, I'll give the anesthetic, prepare the tooth for the crown, and then leave the rest to the auxiliary help, who will take the impressions and make the temporary. The next time I see the patient is to cement the crown and say goodbye!" Nice attitude for a professional health-care individual!

I got to the office at 5:30 the next morning. The reviewers were not expected until 8:00. I inspected the building, which was in a lot better shape than the day before. I also found a group of offices in the back of the first floor that I had missed the day before. I swept the floors, dusted the desks, wiped off the phones, threw away unneeded papers, and did the best I could to make the place presentable.

The examiners arrived precisely at 8:00 and went immediately to the back offices and never left there. They never once went to the second floor. I spent the morning with them and learned a lot of how they think and their attitude toward our company. It turned out to be a favorable encounter in spite of my disappointment that they only reviewed charts and skipped a walk-through of the facility. The office did pass the audit, but this was not known for three months, which is the expected length of time for the committee to submit its report. I was surprised that the DOC doctors were so supportive, and non-punitive.

A similar episode happened in National City. I had previously reviewed the office and found that it was in compliance as far as documentation was concerned. Compliance meant a score of 75 percent or higher. However, there were still issues the office needed to correct. All audited offices received the results of their audits in the form of a corrective action letter, which outlined their deficiencies and stated a re-audit date. The audit score and the type of deficiencies determined the next audit date.

This facility was selected by the DOC to review. I had concerns about the cleanliness of the small lab, which housed the sterilizer, x-ray developing machine, a plaster bin, a plaster trimmer, and dental supplies in an area that was about six feet square. It was a mess. The office had no operating rooms, just partitioned alcoves, which were neat and organized. So I took it upon myself to get to the office at 6:00 the morning of the audit to clean up the lab before the DOC auditor arrived.

The auditor arrived promptly at 9:00 and immediately went into a small office with a desk and an x-ray view box. He never left that room until he was finished. He left without checking the rest of the office, including the spanking clean lab.

◆　　　◆　　　◆

The leading dental consultant in the DOC, Dr. Marvin Erlich, who had created the protocols the DOC uses, often handled some of the DOC audits himself. He was prominent in the DHMO field because he had owned and run a large dental clinic in South Los Angeles. He was a remarkable and interesting man who was near the end of his dental career. I met him at one office in Redlands for a review of that office.

The provider dentist was Chinese, and his wife was working the front desk and performing as his chair-side assistant. He was so proud that he had practiced for fifty years and was still going strong. Together they had an excellent practice and were widely respected in the community.

As usual I got there early to be sure that everything was in compliance. The facility was in an old frame house that matched the older area of Redlands. An empty chiropractic office shared the building; the chiropractor was a relative and was on vacation. They set up the x-ray view box for Dr. Erlich in an empty operating room of the chiropractic office.

It happened again. Dr. Erlich never looked at the office, just the charts and progress notes. He was very slow, and as I sat beside him checking cases, he would doze off. I kept asking, "Are you okay?" He would nod his head so as to assure me he wasn't dead. Apparently he had been quite ill, but I didn't pry, and he didn't volunteer any information. We stopped in the middle of the audit and went across the street for a sandwich. After a really short lunch, we went back to the charts. The office passed with flying colors.

Auditing the Specialists

Around this time, Tony, being extremely concerned about passing DOC examinations, decided we needed to perform specialist audits. There was some concern about me, a general dentist, being accepted by specialists. But Betty and I designed a form that could be used for all the specialties. It worked. I went all over the state auditing orthodontic, pedodontic, periodontic, and oral surgery offices.

Sterilization protocols by most of the orthodontists were terrible. They used mostly cold sterilization solutions, which worked only if the instruments were left in the trays of solutions for twenty-four hours without adding any newly soiled ones. I had lunch with the former president of the California Orthodontic Society, who showed me his facility in Redlands. He had six open, deep trays of cold sterilization solutions, which made up his "sterilization system." Most of the modern orthodontists use autoclave sterilizers that are specifically designed for orthodontic instrumentation.

Another problem with orthodontic offices was the way they set up the treatment chairs. They had small work trays next to the chair with arch wires, pliers, and impression trays sitting in special racks in the open air and easily accessible to the curious hands of the young patients. I took a lot of heat from irate orthodontists because all the changes I suggested they make to come into compliance were costly and would likely increase chair time per patient. Today's orthodontists have improved their treating systems for the protection of the patients and their own protection. The changes were a good thing.

Pedodontic or pediatric dental offices at that time tended to be lax in the way they monitored nitrous oxide sedation. There are mandated protocols in place today that provide protection for children. On occasion, however, a young child will die from this sedation. When I audited a pedodontic facility in the Bay area, I saw a "papoose board" for the first time. This board is used to strap the child into a prone position, limiting extreme movements. It looked to me like a form of torture and a cop-out by the dentist who can't manage a child by using conventional techniques. The toy box worked for me.

I scheduled an appointment with a pedodontic office in Pasadena to perform an audit. It was not an easy place to schedule, but we finally agreed on a time. When I entered the office waiting room, I was stunned by the busyness of the place, the noise, the chaos, and the confusion caused by the little rascals and their parents. The place was obviously overbooked. The pedodontist Dr. Thelma Makemore, was a woman with an attitude and a big ego. Thelma didn't like me and I reciprocated mentally. She showed me the operating rooms and their anesthesia setups. Reluctantly, I gave her a pass for the audit, because a pedodontist was necessary for referrals from our providers in the area.

Later, a child died while under treatment. Dr. Makemore also had problems with Medi-Cal over billing. The state revoked her license, and as a result she is no longer practicing. This was another case of anesthetic misuse by a specialist on a healthy child. The needless death underscored my belief that general anesthesia for dental procedures on kids is ridiculous unless there is a justified medical issue, such as mental retardation or autism.

In contrast, there was a pedodontist in Cerritos, Dr. Blue , who was a great children's dentist because he was a kid himself. He was a tall, slender man who wore Hawaiian shirts and bubbled with enthusiasm. His office was huge and painted with every conceivable color possible. (It was the first time I had ever seen purple toilets.) He also had games for the kids to play while they waited.

I always joked with Dr. Blue about his (ugly) shirts, commenting on how great they looked. So one day he was talking to me when he suddenly excused himself and left in a rush. He quickly returned, smiling, and presented me with the card of his tailor. He actually had those shirts custom-made. I didn't have the heart to tell him what I really thought of those shirts.

Through the years Dr. Blue has been an excellent dentist who has often helped me with problem cases. He is one of the few pedodontists who believes in local anesthesia instead of always knocking the kids out. He never uses a "papoose board."

The first oral surgeon that I faced as an auditor, Dr. Raymond Less, had two offices in Sacramento. One office was in an elaborate two-story brick building across the street from the hospital, and the other across the Fulton street railroad tracks in the southern section of town. His offices were impeccable. He used general anesthetic on practically all his cases. He rarely had to operate in a hospital setting because of the completeness of his operating rooms, his anesthetic delivery systems, and recovery space.

Raymond had become the main recipient of all specialty referrals for the area. Raymond was a money machine who never saw a wisdom tooth he didn't want to extract. My battle with him was over fees and non-covered procedures.

I asked, "What kind of car do you drive, Raymond?"

"A Ferrari".

"See! I rest my case."

"But it is five years old," rationalized Raymond.

The next time I saw him, he took me out to lunch and drove me there in his Chevy. It was at lunch that I noticed what a nervous guy he was. His speech was always so fast that I had to make him repeat what he said, which was always denials of over-billing. However, through many following years, Raymond was always available on short notice from me to handle difficult cases, still driving his Chevy. I never did get a chance to look in his garage.

Before I got involved in the DHMO programs and was still in private practice, I rarely referred my patients to periodontists. The courses I'd taken for continuous education credits left me cold when it came to referring. I performed my own periodontal surgeries and doggedly followed-up on my periodontal delinquents. I had no negative outcomes if my patient's complied with my recommendations.

So, when I audited my first periodontist, I was amazed that he was successful in treating so many cases that appeared hopeless. Dr. Suturn Cutler had an office in Hemet. He was very receptive to my presence and showed me around his office that had five operating rooms, including a recovery area. He was licensed to use general anesthesia, which was usually nitrous oxide. In addition to the five operating rooms, he had four chairs for four hygienists. His documentation and charting were accurate and mostly digital. His follow-ups with his patients and the referring dentists were the best that I had ever seen.

I had only one problem with him—his arrogance. He had a very high opinion of himself and his specialty. My major turn-off came when I read an article by Dr. Cutler in the Hemet News in which he stated that dentists who do not refer their patients to periodontists are guilty of dental malpractice.

It turned out that he was an attorney as well as a dentist.

The Impatient Patient

Access to treatment was always one of the main sticking points of the Knox-Keane legislation. All patients, children and adults alike, must have reasonable access to treatment. All offices by contract have to demonstrate 24-hour availability for emergencies.

When checking any of the providers, I always reviewed the appointment book to see if DHMO patients had the same access to treatment as non-DHMO patients. Many offices scheduled DHMO patients on one day a week and double- or triple-book the appointments. Most offices thought this type of booking was necessary because a lot of DHMO patients missed appointments. When the pain goes away, they just don't bother to show up.

This was always a sticking point in the perception of the quality of treatment DHMO patients received. Many grievances were based on the excessively long waits to be seen. There is always a balancing act between patient compliance and the dentist's ability to make up for missed appointments. In other words, the dentists are not always at fault.

Chapter 9

Up Pops the Devil

I had many roles for DC: auditing providers for quality, recruiting new providers, adjudicating claims, and handling specialty referrals. Then as the company grew, Tony started bringing on more people and establishing separate departments. He hired a pleasant and feisty woman, Keri, who was an old pro in the business of provider relations. We got along great mainly because I laughed at her crude jokes. Keri's only problem was her style when dealing with unhappy providers who needed more solace than abuse. I used to get calls from the provider dentists, whom I had cultivated and befriended, yowling about the acerbic and crude attitude of our new Provider Relations manager. I assured them that DC had their best interests at heart, and I put up with her because she truly was a diamond in the rough. When I finally left DC, Keri was still there but much more subdued. She must have run out of her lousy jokes. Thank God!

Then Tony introduced me to a female dentist, Madge Rose, who was to become the dental director and to whom I would be subservient. At first appearance she conveyed the sweet smell of innocence. The only thing that was missing was a shawl covering her head, which would have given her the appearance of a starving refugee. She was not a bad-looking woman, but she almost immediately turned into a barracuda after Tony gave her a fancy office next to his. She would review my audits of the various providers and critique them while sitting behind her massive mahogany desk.

One time I made the huge mistake, in her view, of using the word *nice* when describing how the office personnel presented themselves. "It was a nice office."

"Dr. Pedersen, never use the word *nice*," she said. "It's an ugly, non-descriptive word!" This was new to me, because it's a word everybody uses. I had never heard that spin on such a word. But this gal really did have a thorn up her posterior.

Madge was an interesting person because of her background. She was born in Poland and immigrated to the United States when she was ten years old. Her father was a very successful biochemist, and they were rich. Madge hated her father, which I could never fathom. Her father had worked for a dental company and developed a dental composite filling material that at that time was used by most of the dentists in America.

She told me of the hardships they endured to get to the United States. As a ten-year-old, Madge had trouble adjusting to the American way of life and finding new friends. She had no problem with English because English was taught in all the Polish schools as a secondary language. I found this to be true when traveling to Europe. All the European elementary schools teach English along with their native languages. It's hard to believe that something similar can't be done in the United States.

Madge went to dental school in Texas and graduated with honors. There is no question that she was an exceptionally smart young doctor. She was married to a young and pleasant medical doctor who was ready to complete his internship. DC headquarters were located in Irvine. Madge lived in Sylmar, which is in the San Fernando Valley. She had a long drive to work but was punctual most of the time. Very few people in the office liked her except for Tony, who always liked the female employees.

Madge wanted to go with me on some of my audits, so I scheduled several offices in the San Fernando Valley. She was immediately upset with my style when having an exit interview with the doctor(s). She would say, "You're too kind to the doctors and staff. They should recognize that we are aware of all their deficiencies, and they need to immediately come into compliance!" She resented their smiles when we left.

She had a different attitude, however, when we visited the last facility, which was operated by Dr. Harry Duggan, who was a friend of hers. This dentist was a pleasant, crusty old-timer. She was upset with me when I showed her how he had failed to diagnose a huge abscess on an upper front tooth. She instructed me to pass that chart anyway. The double standard was alive and well. I passed the chart; giving in to her demands, which went against my standards and made me feel like a wimp.

I explained to Madge that I would have a hard time changing my approach to the providers. I told her that I considered them colleagues who always welcomed my non-punitive approach. I considered myself as more of a teacher to help them handle the complexities associated with complying with the regulations foisted on them by the DHMOs and our need to answer to the DOC. She was not impressed, but kept quiet the rest of the day.

Madge accompanied me on a focused audit of an office in Riverside. She had accused the doctor of not being in compliance with some of the OSHA (Occupational Safety and Health Administration) standards as well as deficient charting of the dental procedures. We spent a lot of time at this office, with Madge trying to intimidate the doctor and me acting as a baffle between them. She wanted to terminate the office, but I managed to convince her that they would mend their ways and comply. I emphasized to her the importance of having a long list of providers for the marketing department when it is competing for contracts.

Going home that day, we stopped for lunch. She asked me if I thought she was a "bitch."

"No question," I answered.

She replied, "Well, I'm rich and I don't care!"

◆　　　◆　　　◆

OSHA played a large role in the regulation and compliance of the dentists who were providers for the state-regulated DHMOs. All practices had to have spill kits for the disposal of toxic wastes, such as mercury. The spill kits consisted of kitty litter, a dust-pan, and brush. The kitty litter would absorb the toxic material—mercury, in this case—and the stuff dumped into a container marked "Toxic."

All dental offices today hire toxic waste disposal companies to handle such issues, including the disposal of x-ray solutions and cold sterilizing agents. Dental offices have to have posted protocols for x-ray protection, appropriate medical emergency kits, and thorough sterilization techniques. This is a good protection for the office personnel as well as the patients.

However, weird outcomes occasionally can result with regulatory government agencies. For example, a respectable old-school dentist suffered the ravages of government paranoia. A nosy fourteen-year-old kid was leaving the office when he opened many of the cabinet drawers. One drawer revealed a small ball of mercury rolling around between some towels. He told his mother, who was a do-gooder, and she immediately called OSHA. This resulted in a speedy response, which is unusual for government agencies. They sent out a four guys in anti-contamination suits and headgear with slit glasses. They charged in like white-clad ninjas and scared the hell out of the dentist, two patients, and his staff. They sprayed the place and told everybody they should not return to the office for a week. Then OSHA charged the dentist $4,000. Our protective government strikes again.

◆　　◆　　◆

The California Association of Dental Plans (CADP) was created in 1985. DC with several of the other plans joined in its formation. They wanted the CADP to lobby the politicos in Sacramento and act as a liaison to the DOC. I called and still do call the CADP a dental version of the United Nations, because everyone at these meetings is always watching carefully what the other companies are doing. Remember, all these DHMO companies were competitors.

Madge and her husband, along with Gloria and I, attended a meeting of the CADP in Indian Wells, California, held at the Grand Champions Hotel. It was quite an experience, with numerous meetings, cocktail parties, and fine food. —Unfortunately, I was the victim of a salmonella attack from the chicken dinner. Man, was I sick. Thanks to Maggie's husband, who tried to help me, I managed to check out of the hotel and head for home. I had the chills so bad that thought I would knock all my teeth out because of non-stop chattering. Gloria drove me to the hospital in Newport Beach. (She hated to drive at night, but she had no choice. She initially headed for Los Angeles by mistake, but she corrected and we ended up in Newport Beach).

This incident showed me that Madge could occasionally have compassion—not a whole lot, but some.

The Epitome of Recruiting

DC was growing at a fast pace, but there was always the problem of getting more provider dentists. Tony came up with what he thought was a foolproof idea that would guarantee an increase in our provider list. He mailed out the plan to *all* the dentists in California, making the ridiculous statement that DC would guarantee that the dentist would make 85 percent of his usual and customary fees. Of course, the response was immense and fast. However, this meant that in order to comply with the regulations, DC would have to perform facility audits of the potential providers as well as ensure appropriate credentialing. (There have been cases of illegal immigrants practicing dentistry in home garages and shacks.)

Many of my snobbish friends always looked down on the idea of a DHMO dentist. They had the idea that if a dentist were a member of the ADA and CDA, he was above reproach. They were always of the opinion that the higher the fee, the better the quality of the work. When I visited some of the dentists who were members of the ADA and CDA and who never had been audited, I found most of them to be out of compliance with the standards set forth by the Knox-Keene laws. Thus, I now had my response to the scoffs of my friends: you can go to your high-priced dentist, but his office would most likely flunk DC examination.

Of course, Tony's grandiose plan failed for many reasons, including the financial feasibility. It just didn't make any sense, but it gave me real insight into the state of the dental profession.

Vacation Mistake

Gloria and I went on a well-earned vacation to Scandinavia. We were gone two weeks on a wonderful motor trip through Denmark, Sweden, and Norway. It was an interesting trip because I visited many dental offices in Sweden and Norway. They were all very modern and clean, with happily crowded waiting rooms. These countries have socialized medicine and dentistry. Everything is free, but one must be a citizen to get treated.

We returned from the trip in the latter part of September 1991. On my first Monday morning back home, I went back to DC headquarters

and was greeted by Tony. He was always cheerful, but this day he had a sad look on his face. He then told me that DC was in the process of being bought by a large medical HMO and I should immediately sell my stock. He was concerned that some of the dealings he had made were not absolutely above reproach.

And, by the way, I was fired! I learned my lesson—don't go on long vacations!

Just prior to Madge's joining the company stage, DC moved to new quarters, which were located just two miles from my home. The previous DC offices were located in Irvine, fifteen miles away. My logistical advantage disappeared in a flash.

Chapter 10

New Challenges

My unemployment lasted only a few months. I had heard that Clinical Dental Systems (CDS) was looking for a dentist who was efficient in the field of recruiting dentists for dental plans. The CEO, Fred Bellwether, was a tall, imposing man who was not a dentist, but he was very sharp and knew the dental business. He offered me a job as an independent contractor. I was to be paid a commission for every dental office that I could find to sign a contract. Even though I was somewhat desperate, the offer did not fit my needs. I lobbied for a salaried job, but Fred was not enthusiastic about the idea (he was the ultimate bean-counter).

My savior appeared when the brother of the dentist who owned the company, Mark, met me and agreed that it would be in my best interests to have a salaried job. The salary was modest, but it was a reliable salary, which removed the pressure that would exist when attempting to sell new ideas to skeptical dentists. My previous experience, especially in the northern part of the state, reminded me of the difficulties and humiliation associated with trying to sell the idea of participating in a DHMO to dentists. Recruiting in northern California was almost like working in a foreign country. Since I started working there, I've thought that California should be two separate states, Northern and Southern California. The populations are just too disparate.

I started my new position as a dental consultant in December 1991. The headquarters of CDS were twenty-two miles away, which was in stark contrast to the location of nearby DC. It was in a large hotel-business building combination, ten stories high, and located in the northern corner of Orange County. CDS was housed in the top two floors. The building was very modern with lots of glass. The offices were open and cheerful, except for some of the people.

I always had interesting conversations with Mark, who gave me considerable insight as to what went on around us. Mark was married, rich, and liked the ladies. He once told me while we were sitting in his glassed-in office that he wanted to see nothing but great-looking ladies in his visual field. It was true. About ten desks were arranged in a large room next to his office, and every desk had a good-looking woman working at her computer. He ultimately got a divorce, and to this day he shares a non-committal life with one of those great looking women.

One day I was sitting in his office while Mark was opening mail. He laughed and showed me a check for $60,000, saying, "Jim, I have no idea what this is for," and laughed. Some people have all the luck!

Mark's personal secretary was named Trudy, an attractive, middle-aged woman who was very kind to me and helped me when I ran into problems. She was so blasé, sitting at her desk just outside Mark's door, answering the phone, attending to his every wish, and even making some of his romantic dates for him. It was amazing how skillfully she worked with Mark and Fred, who were constantly wheeling and dealing and changing their plans minute by minute.

Chapter 11

The CDS Setup

CDS was not wholly a DHMO company like Den-Cap (DC). It was a family-owned large credit operation that had, at that time, forty-three dental centers that were run by managing dentists. CDS accounted for only a part of the family business, which was primarily real estate. The family also owned the hotel and business building in which CDS was housed.

The company owned the dental centers, which usually had two or three dentists in addition to the managing dentist. The managing dentists were paid a percentage of the gross business. With this percentage they had to pay the associate dentists, the support personnel, and the operating costs. The company employed an operations director, Dr. John Alden, Mark's nephew, and regional dental directors, who were all dentists

The main goal of the company was to own at least one hundred California dental centers before the end of the century. In order to expand into other areas, the company had to obtain signed DHMO contracts with other general dentists and specialists in a specific city or town and surrounding areas, called "service areas." Once these contracts were in place, the company could submit the documentation to the Department of Corporations (DOC) for its approval to allow CDS to open a dental center for that service area. Thus, CDS was trying to expand its number of dental clinics using its DHMO ties. The company has always considered the DHMO programs as stepping-stones to the much more profitable clinics.

I considered the clinics post-graduate dental schools because new graduates were hired and thrown into a dental practice that demanded production and the completing of restorative work in a fraction of the time they took in dental school. It was not pretty to watch all the daily

corrections of poorly completed work. While I was reviewing one of the centers, I spent a few moments with one of the young female dentists, Dr. Tran Nguyen, who had been with CDS for about six months. I asked her, "How do you like working here?"

"It's been wonderful, but demanding," she answered. "I really am improving in my timing, and my fillings are beginning to stay in!"

◆   ◆   ◆

CDS did have a marketing department, which managed the television and radio advertising of the clinics. In order to expand its benefit options, CDS offered a DHMO plan along with the State-funded Denti-Cal program. Denti-Cal was a large part of the CDS book of business.

There was no question that CDS was a dental business centered in their clinics and their no-interest credit contracts. Because of CDS, a lot of people received dental treatment that they never would have if it weren't for its liberal credit policies. For this reason, the DOC was very frustrated because its tough watchdog policies appeared to be attempts to put CDS out of business and would, in effect, shut off access to dental care for many low-income families.

My main task from the beginning was to recruit dental providers and specialists in order to obtain control of a given service area. My first challenge was Sacramento.

While I was preparing to go to northern California, the DOC was performing a quality audit on four selected centers. One center in downtown Los Angeles was being scrutinized by a team of dentists from the faculty at UCLA representing the DOC. I went there to see how the examiners operated and hopefully become friends with them. I could make my phone calls and appointments with the Sacramento dentists and also be available for any questions from them. It was kind of a baptism of fire.

I was called in by one of the examiners to look at a case. He showed me the chart and the x-rays. The dentist had diagnosed the case for ten full crowns on a mouth that, according to the x-rays, had no visible cavities. For once I was at a loss for words. Just at that time, John appeared to see how things were going. I showed him the x-rays. John was normally a master of bailing out poor-performing dentists, but in this case he was also at a loss for words.

We called in the diagnosing dentist, who was a young Asian, and confronted him with the case. He answered, "That's the way we do it in China!" He was immediately taken aside by John and disciplined. It has always been company policy that dentists who make mistakes in diagnosis and treatment are penalized financially.

Debbie McConnell and the DOC

Debbie was the leader of the DOC team when reviewing compliance by CDS. She was one of the scariest people I've ever encountered. She was very pale with dark black hair and piercing green eyes. She always wore a dark black suit, and she smelled. She must have never cleaned that suit. Every time I saw her, she wore the same suit. She would smugly sit at the meetings with her note pads and later a laptop, and I just knew that she was conjuring up some new deficiency to test our mettle. She had been overheard saying that she intended to put CDS out of business. It never happened, but she scared the hell out of all of us with her destructive dedication.

When she announced she was coming, you could see the complete panic at headquarters. People scurried all over the place, collecting documents and preparing responses to any new deficiencies that Debbie could find. It was a mess, but in the end, CDS somehow survived.

Debbie had left the DOC by the time the Department of Managed Health Care (DHMC) was formed in 2000 to remove jurisdiction of all HMOs from the DOC. Thank God!

Chapter 12

No Go in Sacramento

I spent the first two weeks of December 1991 in a rainy Sacramento. I had not been in Sacramento for at least twenty years. Back then the city had no freeways, so even with the help of my trusty Thomas Guide in the "basic" rental car, finding my way around the city two decades later was a real challenge. Getting lost was easy. Sacramento extends along the American and Sacramento rivers, which cross the area on the diagonal. Figuring out north-south streets was really tough, and east-west streets even harder. In addition, the old part of Sacramento, which houses the beautiful Capitol, was enclosed by a loop of freeways, including "Business 80." Trying to find my way around to unfamiliar addresses, always being pressed by impatient, tailgating maniac drivers, tested my fortitude, religion, and language.

My two weeks were well spent. My hard work and "BS" got commitments from fifty-one providers. The main reason the company wanted these providers was that it was thinking of approaching a large group. As was the case with DC, in order to get a contract with a large group, CDS marketing had to demonstrate to the group's HR management that it had a large number of providers who were located in convenient, accessible regions. They also had to come up with a better deal than the competing DHMOs by offering more comprehensive benefits. In addition, with a sanction from the DOC for the creation of clinics (staff models), CDS had leases on one downtown office space, one lease on a space in south Sacramento, one in north Sacramento, and plans to build a dental center from scratch in midtown. With such a large panel of providers, CDS could make an offer nobody could refuse.

I was candid with all the potential providers, explaining that the deal had not yet been completed. If the deal did not come to pass, they were under no obligation to stay with the plan, and the agreements they signed were not binding.

Unfortunately, the deal did not go through. What irritated me most was the casual attitude of management. The operations director, John, who through the years was always a close and understanding friend, conveyed his sympathy and thanked me for a job well done.

Ironically, many of the providers stayed on even though they had no enrollees at that time. Later, things would change for the better.

Chapter 13

Santa Barbara and San Luis Obispo Counties

Fred called me to go over some of his plans for adding to the number of dental centers. He explained the demographics involved in their thinking for finding successful spots for the centers. The main idea was to find an area that was roughly five square miles in area with a population, mostly Hispanic, of about fifty thousand. They usually looked at existing buildings they could lease and convert to dental usage. The most common buildings they found were old bank buildings. They consulted with several building engineers and then drew plans for the layouts of the centers.

As with my previous company, I always questioned why management never consulted a dentist when they were planning these offices. This non-professional approach many times resulted in curious, non-functional layouts that required considerable revamping after the fact. As usual, management was always cost-conscious, which resulted in buying dental equipment that was in constant need of repair.

Two consultants worked with the office planners to set up the new facilities. Belinda handled the furnishings, colors, pictures, and the initial setups of the centers. Patricia was a hygienist who was responsible for the sterilization setups, x-ray regulations compliance, and dental operating room layouts. Belinda was the feisty one, while Patricia was more serious. They were both excellent at their positions. When they were finished, the centers looked well appointed, with colors that carried out the CDS corporate theme.

I had to go to Santa Maria and contract general dentists to be providers for the CDS HMO products. As before, once the required general dentists and specialists were signed, CDS could apply to the

DOC for that particular service area. Santa Maria, Lompoc, and Santa Barbara became part of the CDS network with dental centers located in areas with large Hispanic populations, mostly on Denti-Cal.

San Luis Obispo is a beautiful college town located in a valley that is formed on the west by the Santa Lucia Mountains, which separate it from the Pacific Ocean. On the ocean side of the mountains is the famous Hearst Castle. The town itself is famous for the Madonna Inn, which is the home of the world's most ornate restrooms. My challenge was obtaining a contract from a dentist with a huge ego and a beautiful office that had views of the surrounding valley and its vineyards. He did sign with us, but I spent many hours over the years on the phone with him and his complaints about our low capitation rates. He would drop the plans and then sign on again. He was a pain, but we needed him in that area. CDS never built a center there. Here was a case where the demographics in that area did not square with the CDS format.

The Santa Maria office was fun because the dentist was a big bear of a man with a gruff, almost scary way about him. He gave me a real bad time asking tough questions, which I nervously parried with answers that were honest and forthright. His sour face then changed into a smile, and he agreed to contract with us. I could never understand why he signed because he was already overly busy. We were lucky because he was a fine dentist.

The Lompoc office was close to Vandenberg Air Force Base and had a lot of military families as patients. Lompoc is pure Americana, a small town with lots of trees and old houses of early 1900s vintage. One of those old houses had been converted to a dental office, which was quaint and homey by design. This office took us on almost as a favor because it was so busy. The office was vital to CDS because of its location and the lack of providers in the area. The dentist was a big, grumpy man almost akin to the Santa Maria dentist, but friendlier. So another contract was signed after my sanguine prodding.

Gloria and I stayed in a small, inexpensive hotel in nearby Solvang. Solvang was a small, touristy village that was a combination of the Old World Danish lifestyle and the wine-growing ranch-like atmosphere of rural Santa Barbara County. At the turnoff from the highway was a small village called Buellton, which was famous as the home of Andersen's Pea Soup Restaurant. There was also the nearby town of Los Olivos, which was surrounded by acres and acres of well-kept vineyards. Just a few miles down the road was the immense ranch of Michael Jackson, whose gated entrance was always crowded by Jackson worshipers. I had no luck finding a provider for this area, whose rich ranchers, horsemen, and vintners financially took care of the dental needs of their lower income workers.

We stayed in Santa Barbara for a few days in a Best Western Hotel. My efforts there were successful in that I contracted several dental groups in the city as well as in nearby Goleta. We traveled south to Ventura and Oxnard and visited the CDS centers that were already operating.

The Oxnard office was old and small but very busy. It was successful because the demographics of the area matched Fred's formula: lots of low-income Hispanics. The managing dentist was an aggressive little guy whom I called the "Mad Russian." He produced a lot of dental work and a lot of complaints, which were usually over his personality and eccentric mannerisms. It was not unusual for him to follow an aghast patient after he had dismissed him to the appointment desk, shouting, yelling instructions, and scheduling the next appointment. His dentistry was fairly acceptable, in spite of his intensity. How he kept patients coming back is a tribute to his work. .

Oxnard was next to the U.S. Naval Construction Battalion Station at Port Hueneme. This group used many of the CDS-contracted providers in the surrounding area, which was an encouraging statistic for the DHMO business.

The Ventura clinic was never a real winner, probably due to the layout and design by the non-dentists of the company that resulted in an extremely patient-unfriendly appearance, despite the heroic efforts of Belinda and Patricia. Patients had to walk through the back of a market from the parking lot to access the entrance, which was at the end of a long, barren hallway. The entry to the waiting room was always cluttered with families of the patients standing around impatiently with their little kids running noisily around, eating, and generally making a mess. There was always an aura of negativism around that nut house. I'm not sure, but the office was probably closed.

Chapter 14

The Bay Area

I spent a lot of time in northern California recruiting providers in order to obtain approved service areas from the DOC. I lined up the usual reluctant specialists and many general dentists from as far north as Santa Rosa, as far south as Monterey, and as far to the east as Stockton. The specialists were the main problem because they were reluctant to sign any type of contract. Their attitudes were strange because I stressed that the contracts were non-binding and were a means for specialty referrals. Some of the specialists did not want have anything to do with DHMOs. So we used what was called a "unilateral contract." I worked with Sherry in the office to create these contracts, which (sneaky, but effective), which, to my knowledge were okay with the DOC. None of the adamant specialists were on our list. The issue never came up during the DOC audits of the company, so I kept my big mouth shut.

The San Francisco Bay area has to be one of the most beautiful areas in the world. The Golden Gate Bridge and the Bay Bridge connect San Francisco to the many cities that border the San Francisco Bay. San Francisco is a fantastic combination of exotic, tall buildings and residential sections made up of narrow houses with no easements and painted with in loud colors. And watching the commuters get out of cable cars at the Powell Street turnaround, and the driver then aim the car back up the street to Knob Hill is an unforgettable sight.

The 450 Sutter Medical Building on Post Street in San Francisco is more than forty stories tall and a medical city within itself. The dental offices were all very small in square footage because of the design of the building and because of the extraordinarily expensive rents. Most waiting rooms were limited to a few chairs and magazine racks containing issues from bygone days. The business office had room for a desk, an appointment book, and a phone. The lab was usually the dark room, storage room, and sterilizing area in a space the size of a small wardrobe closet. The dentists represented every possible culture and nationality. Office decors ranged from modern to Oriental. And parking? Good luck! Nobody validated, so being a member of a DHMO didn't keep the costs of dentistry down for the patients.

The Mission District is a collection of old buildings with signs covering all the walls, sidewalks that are sticky with gum waste, human derelicts standing on the corners hawking for handouts, tram bells clanging, smelly buses blocking the intersections, and second floor dental offices all over the place. Parking is a challenge. When you found a parking space, you always hoped your car would still be there when you returned.

One dental office that signed with me was exceptionally large with a huge clientele. It was like a Greyhound Bus station with waiting rooms here and there, a large business office, and appointment desk. This was the ideal capitation office because of the volume and types of patients. The owner/dentist was Dr. Russell Camillo, who was very likeable and wealthy. He also was an inventor who had many patents on toothbrushes and dental instruments. He designed a brush that would brush all your teeth with one swipe. It was large and totally impractical, but he was really proud of his invention. He gave me one, which I tried—it hurt!

We became good friends through the years. When I was in town, he would take me to lunch at the San Francisco Country Club in his Corvette. I didn't see much of the scenery because his driving invited closed eyes and prayer. He was a little old to drive such a vehicle, but he loved that car and would never part with it, except maybe for a new one.

The clubhouse where we had lunch was built before the 1906 earthquake and had survived. It was loaded with tradition. The view of the course from the dining room was spectacular. The rolling hillside with old oak trees and cypress trees shaped by the winds from the ocean, the view of Lake Merced, and the manicured fairways, afforded a wonderful and relaxing luncheon date with an old friend.

Russell also had a more modern and sophisticated office along the 280 freeway in South San Francisco. It was on the top floor of a modern medical-dental building with a spectacular view of South San Francisco and Daly City. Its marble and glass interior contained the latest and most expensive dental equipment. This was in sharp contrast with his Mission District office, but generated nowhere near the income. This was a good office for the CDS DHMO program because it added a touch of class to our act, and it gave him additional patients. Russell was also very helpful as a consultant for the area. He knew everybody, which opened a lot of recruiting doors for me.

CDS opened a center on Mission Street a few blocks south of Russell's large office. It was a one-story version of his facility. It was near a corner McDonald's and a few small nondescript stores. This was derelict canyon, but the center was always busy. The office's main problem was that everything was always breaking down, from the dental units to the air conditioning. The center had replaced a defunct Italian restaurant. The kitchen vents actually worked quite well to evacuate the fumes from the Harvey Chemiclave sterilizers, which were the mainstay of all the centers. Harveys use an alcohol-based compound to generate the heat sufficient to knock out all spores and bacteria. Rarely did the centers use steam autoclaves, which were more expensive, but better, in my opinion. The Harveys were easy to use and monitor for the mostly rookie staffs of the centers. The layout was atrocious, with a zigzag hallway between the operating cubicles. The waiting "room" had no definite boundaries.

Every time I visited the Mission Street center, the staff and the dentists were wonderful to work with. They never complained in spite of the ever-present mechanical malfunctions. The patient load came from the lowest level of the wage scale, but the center always made a profit.

On one occasion, I conducted a recruiting session at the University of California Dental School on Parnassus Avenue in San Francisco to encourage future graduates to work for CDS. The school building features a lot of glass, which ensures fantastic views of the Golden Gate Bridge and surroundings. Our Bay Area rep for CDS had set up the tables in a large conference hall of the school. She also had arranged for soft drinks, sandwiches, and desserts for the students to enjoy while listening to the CDS pitch. We had one problem: CDS banners were supposed to have been sent along with the other goodies, such as CDS ballpoint pens and money clips. This prompted me to go by the Mission Center to see if they had anything we could use. Voila! They had some

CDS signs stashed away that we found and freshened up. They worked perfectly. The session was held at 3:00 PM, and we invited all the junior and senior students to attend. It was neat to be able to talk with the enthusiastic students and extol the virtues of getting started with CDS. The classes were ethnic mixtures of young men and women. Man, they looked like babies!

Remember, this was northern California, where anti-DHMO bias was still flourishing. It was a very satisfying session because we received commitments from several senior students and many potential ones as well. One of the great selling points of CDS is that the new grads can hit the ground running, making good money while still learning. Such work would help them in paying their huge college loans. Often, many would start their own practices after working two years for CDS, and they became darned good dentists.

That says a lot for the CDS post-graduate dental school.

Setting Up New Centers

As mentioned before, CDS hunted around for existing structures for their centers. Fred found two sites, one in downtown San Francisco and one in downtown Oakland, that were very old but still active advertising dental offices that specialized in full dentures. Both facilities were still managed by the trustees of the estate of Dr. Jason Lowery, who had passed away. CDS closed them for remodeling after signing leases with the estate.

I went with Patricia and Belinda to the Oakland facility. It dated back to 1903 (before the earthquake of 1906) and occupied three stories of an old building stuck between modern buildings in the downtown area, The first floor had about seven operating rooms on one side of a long hallway. None of the rooms had sinks. There was one sink for hand washing about halfway down the hallway on the wall opposite the operating rooms. The dental lab was at the end of the hall next to the only restroom. The lab was a large room with an extra-high ceiling. It was a mess. There was plaster all over the walls and even on the ceiling. The workbenches were covered with old wax residue and plaster. The polishing lathes and polishing wheels were covered with old pumice and polishing rouge. There was no sterilization capability in the entire office.

The second floor was mostly offices and a lunchroom. It appeared that nobody had filed anything for the last fifty years. Then we went up the wooden staircase to the third floor. This floor housed all the dental records going back to 1903. It looked just like a set for a horror movie. Cobwebs, dirt, dust, and a musty smell reminded us of what the old days must have been like. A patient's record was one 3" x 5" lined card with the name and age of the patient and a few lines describing the treatment.

It was Belinda and Patricia's job to supervise the conversion to a functioning dental center. The office opened about six months later. The managing dentist of the old facility stayed on under contract with CDS. He had worked for many years making nothing but full dentures, a technique that is not stressed as much in dental schools today. He helped the new dentists when denture cases came along, which minimized complaints.

The opening day was wild. There was a queue of former denture patients clear around the block waiting for the opening.

The place looked great, though it still had a few problems. One was the size of the operating rooms. They were too small for modern dental chairs. The chairs were set at an angle, but the patient's head was still in the hall. Also, there was still just one sink on the wall for the doctors to wash their hands. There were no sinks in the operating rooms, so if a patient had to rinse and spit, he had to get out of the chair and go to the hall sink or the restroom sink, hopefully unoccupied. Again, this situation could have been avoided if a dentist had been consulted while the management team was making the plans for the office. I'm still baffled that they never took advantage of my services in that regard.

It wasn't long before Fred found a bank office on the main street of Oakland that was more adaptable to the needs of a CDS center. So after about two years, the center moved to the new quarters, which were much better, but still set up without my consultation. However, its location was better because it faced the street and invited walk-ins.

◆　　　◆　　　◆

Then came the remodeling of the old denture office on Market Street in San Francisco. This place was even more fun. Like the Oakland office, this old building had survived the 1906 earthquake. It was old with limited exposure to Market Street at the entrance and ringed by vagrants. The waiting room and business office were quite small, and then the floor plan wandered through a zigzag hallway to a larger rear area. The place appeared to have been an old restaurant before it was a dental office. But it turns out that the restaurant had been a front because in the back there was an entrance that went downstairs to a huge, catacomb-like area that extended hundreds of feet under the adjoining buildings. Legend has it that this was a house of ill repute. The catacombs made a wonderful storage area and lunchroom.

The problem with the location on the corner of a Market Street intersection is that it made the office vulnerable to all sorts of loiterers and in some cases burglars. (This was a problem for many centers located where drug use was rampant in the community.) One day a raving, naked man ran through the door to the Market Street center back to the operating rooms, broke the locks to get to the restroom, and tried to commit suicide. The receptionist called the police, who were always nearby and escorted the poor soul to the slammer.

Parking for the center was always difficult, but most of the patients came by bus or trolley. A small parking lot in the rear was available and had two handicap parking spaces. From this small spot one could get a view of the spectacular city hall, opera house, and conference buildings. Across the street was an expansive park. It always had small, covered kiosks with poorly clad vendors selling all kinds of wares—flowers, souvenirs, drugs, etc. What a city!

◆　　　◆　　　◆

Hayward is a large city south of Oakland on the East Bay. I visited the CDS dentist for the second time, the first being when he signed with Den-Cap. His office was located on a main north-south thoroughfare near the heart of the business area. Dr. Cleveland Tannenbaum owned the building that housed his office and a non-descript rental next door. The place was weird, he was weird, but he was contracted with all the plans. He considered himself the guru of the DHMO field and was not short on ego. He would argue over any quality issues that came up. He also considered himself an expert in the quality management field and made sure that everyone knew of his expertise.

Cleveland was always ready to battle me down to the last detail over any grievance case that would arise, always spouting that he was being singled out for poor quality of treatment when he felt that his work was beyond reproach. His staff privately disliked him intensely. Cleveland was indirectly a great help to me in securing this service area. Subsequently, CDS set up a center in a more central area that could service a considerable number of enrollees, but Cleveland still stayed on the panel, much to my chagrin.

◆　　◆　　◆

CDS succeeded in opening centers all through the Bay Area, while I kept adding new DHMO practices and specialties. For many years, Gloria and I would fly to San Jose and stay at a hotel while I performed audits of private, general dental offices. I rarely would perform a quality audit of one of the CDS centers. CDS had regional dental directors who were available to check the quality as well as the production of the centers. Later on in 1993 I did perform audits of some of the centers. Auditing a private provider facility usually took about two hours, including the exit interview with the doctor. Auditing a center was an all-day job because of the large number of dentists and patients, the additional evaluation of the fees and financial contracts, and a detailed report I had to write for management.

My visits to the centers were very rewarding for me because I could work with the new grads and help them with diagnosis and treatment planning. They were so green and under such pressure. They needed encouragement once in a while amidst the routine demands for production.

Chapter 15

Geographic Managed Care

The concept of a DHMO-type Medi-Cal program had been in the works for many years. A pilot program was tested in Sacramento County through which a DHMO had an arrangement with the state. It was called Geographic Managed Care (GMC). The state would pay a premium to the participating plan per patient. It was called a premium, but really was a capitation. The plan would assign patients to each participating provider dentist and pay him/her a capitation. The capitation was based on the amount of premium received by the plan after deductions for operating expenses and profit.

Four companies, including CDS, were accepted for participation in the one-year test. The two biggest players in the deal were CDS and a company named Acceptable Dental Services (ADS). One small company that participated did so because of a political deal, since the owner had been a supervisor for Sacramento County. I had heard a lot about him from my old friend, Dr. O'Reilly, who was still around even though he had sold his East Sacramento office and was working part-time for a Russian dentist, whom I had recruited earlier.

CDS's part in the GMC program was administered from the beginning by Andrew Drakitz, a bright young fellow from Michigan. He was a master of the computer and worked with me on handling my recruited dental offices. I learned a lot about statistics from him. It was important for CDS to manage the GMC program in a manner that would satisfy the state regulators and the company's fiscal management. It also had to make financial sense to the provider dentists. There were constant communications with the state regarding utilization and access issues, which is where Andrew came in. He would produce a utilization report that compared the fees the dentist would make under Medi-Cal and what the dentist would make under the GMC program. The GMC program was much more financially successful for the dentist than the Medi-cal program.

However, I asked Andrew if he could make any statistical report do what he wanted it to do. He grinned and said, "Yes." But then he explained that statistics are not rigged, but can be subject to all kinds of interpretations by statisticians. The statistics were used to show the providers that they were making more money than their Medicaid counterparts. Actually, four offices lost money on the program—all four were the CDS clinics! I reviewed the data and found the young CDS dentists were over-diagnosing and planning treatments that involved full-mouth reconstruction and the like, which were financial losers. Statistical outcomes in many cases ensured appropriate types of treatments that were financial benefits for the patients and fair reimbursements for the dentists.

The GMC providers because of my efforts had signed up with CDS with one exception. The providers I had recruited knew me and trusted me. I knew them on a first-name basis. One big recruiting problem remained. For some unknown reason I hadn't been able to get the trust of the Vietnamese offices to sign up for the program. I sensed it was a language barrier. So I finally solved the problem by having one member of the CDS staff, a young Vietnamese female dentist named Dr. Tran, meet me in Sacramento and tour the Vietnamese prospects. When we went to each office, it was like old home week for her and the other dentists as they exchanged hugs and kisses. She apparently knew most of them from the old days in Vietnam. One of the offices would not give me the right time of day except for the dentist's wife, who worked the front desk. But she could never get her husband to talk to me. Enter Dr. Tran. My elusive prey immediately came up to me smiling and asked, "Which offices do you need?" I gave my list to the former elusive doctor. He phoned. They all signed on the dotted line! It seemed like I had found the capo of the Vietnamese Dental Mafia! Thanks to Dr. Tran, I completed my list of GMC providers.

I signed one Vietnamese dentist, Dr. Phat, who was probably the worst dentist I had ever seen. His facility was in a Vietnamese strip mall next to a large Asian market and a Vietnamese restaurant. The whole area had an aroma that turned my olfactory sense to mush. The first time I visited Dr. Phat was around lunchtime. He was very friendly, but his gums bled when he smiled. His office had that familiar aroma. That aroma emanated from his lab--he was cooking his lunch in his sterilizer!

His patient charts were completely hopeless. His treatment plans were written in pencil on notebook paper. I found that he took the x-rays home and had his wife arrange them for viewing. I could never understand why there were no grievances against this guy. Then came the light! It turns out that he owned a lot of rental housing, and all his patients lived in them. He was terminated as a provider.

◆　　　◆　　　◆

Sacramento is a multi-cultural area, especially dentally. As mentioned previously, there is a large Vietnamese population in the southern area of Sacramento. Downtown has a large population of Chinese and Iranians. To the north and west there is huge conclave of Russians. Scattered through the whole area are a lot of Indians (Hindu) and Sikhs. Included along the middle area in the south are the Filipinos. They're fun because usually they are very slight people in stature, but have the biggest diplomas I've ever noticed hanging on their office paneling. The parchments are laced with huge swirls and flourishes that give the impression of the Distinguished Service Medal. CDS's list of providers produced a plethora of unpronounceable surnames.

I met with a young Russian dentist who had an office in West Sacramento and was one of the GMC providers. He was a handsome young man, tall and dark. He had graduated from the University of Moscow Dental School and had been a citizen of the United States for the last seven years. After completing his review, we sat down and went over some of his deficiencies (which were few and minor), and then I asked, "What do think of the USA?"

"The USA is the best country in the world, except for one thing," he replied.

"One thing? And what is that?"

"The USA has too many freedoms."

I gulped, smiled, and thanked him for his input. It was certainly food for thought, especially at a time when so many American flags were being burned.

Chapter 16

Upheaval at CDS

My years of my employment at CDS were an exciting period during which I witnessed the internal feuding with awe. In my wildest imagination, I never could dream of such chaos.

As mentioned before, the family-owned company was divided into two parts: CDS and a real estate company. I never completely understood all what was going on, except I knew that Fred was gone. The company was undergoing an investigation by both the DOC and the State Board of California. It hired an attorney, Sheldon Greenblatt, as the new CEO to manage the bailout. The place was a mess, with attorneys everywhere and the staff working feverishly to comply with the demands of the investigators. It was costing a lot of money, but the family wealth could take the hit.

Sheldon was a real work of art. There was no question about his abilities. We all knew that when all the investigations were completed, CDS would emerge the winner because of his genius. Sheldon was a workaholic, never getting more than three hours sleep a night and with a variety of intimate partners plus his wife. He hired other supporters, including a new chief financial officer (CFO), Joe Huang, who was pretty much a shill for his policies. The former CFO was gone. Fred was gone. Mark was gone. John was gone.

Sheldon's right-hand man turned out to be Andrew Drakitz, who had the patience of Job when dealing with him. Everyone could hear Sheldon's rampages, usually at the expense of Andrew. Several of the regional directors, who were very attractive female Iranian dentists, along with Dr. Assad Sumac (the only guy), made up Sheldon's inner circle. They would often have closed meetings, which usually resulted in some new policy that would enhance economic gains. The name of the game was production. Each dental center had to produce. Remember, most of the dentists who worked in the centers were new-grads. In dental school it was not unusual to take two or three hours to make an amalgam filling. At the centers, the dentists were expected to produce possibly ten amalgam fillings on the same patient in less than one hour. The regional directors oversaw the centers and made periodic visits to check the books and prod the dentists for more production. Some treatment outcomes were horrific and resulted in frequent re-treatments and/or grievances. Hence, Sheldon's frequent pep talks, which were quite loud, and could be heard all over the place. Sheldon was a master at degradation of anyone who might slightly suggest a difference of opinion. No excuses!

Along with all these changes in personnel, Sheldon appointed a new dental director, who would be my boss. She was an ambitious Jewish dentist, Dr. Glenda Gold, who had previously worked in one of the centers with John. In retrospect, I think Sheldon had met his match in Glenda.

At this time I was passed over for the assistant dental director's job when Sheldon hired Dr. Jim Wagner for that position. Perhaps Sheldon didn't like me because I still hung onto ideas like integrity and honesty. Sheldon probably made a mistake, because Jim had ideals similar to mine. Jim was a part-timer because he was in the Air Force Dental Corps and in charge of its dental clinic at March Air Force Base in Riverside. He was a pleasant gentleman, and we became close friends. I worked with him on many of the grievance issues and helped with regulatory compliance.

He was the fastest typist on the keyboard I'd ever seen. I asked him why he was so good. He explained that he was raised on a small farm in Ohio along with four brothers and a sister in a two-bedroom house. He was the youngest brother, and when his mother died, he was pretty much the head of the household because his dad was busy with their small gas station located at the entrance to the farm. While going to dental school he would work in the station in his spare time and type on an early computer keyboard. This apparently was the reason he became so proficient.

Jim had been married, but lost his wife of two years in a tragic auto accident. He never married again. He was a handsome dude who attracted many excited glances from the female staff. He would spend a lot of time with Gloria and me at our home, probably because he was so lonely. We used to have long discussions late into the early morning hours about CDS and all the crazy things that went on, especially about Sheldon and Glenda.

I often filled in for Jim while he was on assignment at the Air Force Dental Clinic. He also participated in dental groups that would go to places such as Guatemala and Honduras to do some dentistry, but mostly extractions on the poor populations of the area. He described the awful conditions in which the poor people lived--so much poverty. They lived in huts. The roads were mud. The rain never ceased. The doctors could bring only so much equipment, which limited the dental procedures to surgery and elimination of pain and infection.

◆　　◆　　◆

The company held two types of quarterly meetings. The first was a meeting attended by all the regional dental directors, marketing people, Sheldon, his secretary, Glenda, Jim, and me.

The second meeting was for Quality Management (QM). This meeting was very important and usually a lot of fun. CDS had other consultants on staff in attendance. They would even fly in Dr. Nelson Doby from New York. He had written a QM manual, which was the accepted dental bible used by CDS as the last word in QM. Also attending these meetings was another in-house consultant, Dr. Jason Michaelian, who specialized in compliance with the regulatory agencies was very bright, and homosexual. I never had a problem with Jason, who was very effeminate in his mannerisms. He was the classic mother's boy, but he really knew the business. However, at the meetings he would get into shouting matches with Glenda. She was the shouter, as Jason's quiet demeanor affected her like a drip of water. He would always bring up a subject that had no real relevance to the agenda and with his monotone voice continuously interrupt Glenda to make one inane point after another. Glenda would turn a remarkable magenta shade. Sheldon would occasionally stop by and sit in on the meeting, stay for a few minutes, ask a dumb question, and then leave—to the collective sigh of relief from the board members.

I had been responsible for the makeup of the QM board, so I had carefully selected good dentists from the various specialties, including an oral surgeon, a periodontist, and an endodontist, to attend the meetings. Along with them, I had acquired a close friend of mine from Sacramento, Dr. George Miller, who had a large office in Rancho Cordova and had had experience consulting with Omega Dental. George also had a female pedodontist in his office. She was very helpful to me when I had to handle referrals of kids. She did not use general anesthetic, in contrast to its use by the price-gouging pedodontists.

I spent time with one of the Sacramento pedodontic gougers, Dr. Carlos Sandos, and watched as the roving anesthesiologist, who charged extra for his services, knock out a two-year-old while Carlos put stainless steel crowns on the baby's upper front teeth. The baby was still out and as limp as a rag after forty-five minutes. It was really depressing to see this operation; but these babies are victims of extremely poor parenting. The mothers put their kids to sleep with a bottle of apple juice or the like. They develop what has been called "baby bottle syndrome." It's still amazes me that with all the information that is put out by the media and the American Dental Association that there is so much avoidable rampant tooth decay in kids.

I would pick up George at the airport early in the morning. He couldn't wait to watch the Glenda-Jason act.

Dr. Doby was the dental guru. Everybody looked up to him for his dental sagacity. He was a short, stocky guy who was not the prime example of sartorial splendor because his shirt was never tucked in, his tie never tied, and he never wore socks. He also had one slight problem--he was a narcoleptic. I would be sitting there talking with him, and his eyes were wide open, but he was snoring! When alert, he contributed greatly to the QM management program. Most of his work has carried over into the CADP paradigm. For many subsequent years, I have been in contact with him because of his continuing extensive research and new concepts. He gradually fell away from the picture mainly because of Sheldon's obvious dislike of him. This dislike had to stem from Nelson's honesty and his accuracy in revealing Sheldon's lack of professionalism. Also, he was being paid by CDS $20,000 per visit in addition to paying for his flights to and from Albany, New York, his lodgings, and his meals, which were enormous.

Sheldon's disdain for QM continually irritated Glenda. His problem with the department was that it represented the enemy to the company's bottom line and generated no income. So Glenda countered with the idea of corrective seminars for providers who were dogged by grievances. She would have them come to CDS headquarters and spend several hours of instruction in quality for a fee. For example, a dentist in Pasadena had a huge practice but was always having complaints over fees and quality. He did have a huge ego, but acquiesced to take the course to the tune of $3,000. Therefore, QM became a profit-making department, much to the chagrin of Sheldon. Score a point for Dr. Glenda.

In the small world department, another of Glenda's "students" turned out to be Dr. Duggan, Madge's old friend from DC days. He was the one who missed the huge abscess, which Madge had excused. He spent $3,000 with CDS to review appropriate dental diagnosis. Apparently he finally realized that he had a few shortcomings when reading x-rays. My judgment about him was vindicated.

I miss Madge in a perverse sort of way. She had been such a thorn in my side that I think it actually inured me to the later rants and ravings of Sheldon. It taught me not to take things personally. Even though he hinted about the tenuous status of my job, I knew he was reticent to admit that I was doing a good job. It helped to know that he treated everybody in same deprecating way.

Chapter 17

Donations

Sheldon had managed to square things with the DOC. One stipulation of the settlement was that CDS would have to distribute $489,000 in donations to the three private dentals schools in California. These donations were in lieu of financial penalties. This meant that Sheldon would have to deliver a check for $163,000.00 to each dental school.

The University of Southern California School of Dentistry (USC) was the first stop. Sheldon drove to the dental school to meet with the dean and present the check. Glenda, Andrew, and I accompanied him to the meeting. The dean was very pleasant and accepted the check with gusto. Things went okay except that the professor of Dental Ethics was also present. He lit into us about how shameless the clinics were because they had new graduates performing procedures in impractical lengths of time. The clinics advertised and financed treatments. I couldn't keep quiet and asked him if he had ever practiced clinically before. "No," he said. The smile from the dean told me all I needed to know. Of course, he had no idea that CDS offered treatment at no-interest financing and provided dental treatment to thousands of patients who probably would otherwise go untreated.

It was true that the new grads had to produce at a faster rate than at school, but it is interesting to note that their quality did not generate many grievances. (The experience of the young female dentist whose fillings fell out at first was more the exception than the rule.) Financial issues were usually the main sources of grievances. Remember, most of the CDS clientele were low-income families. And after these young dentists worked for two or more years at CDS and went out on their own, they became very successful. Many of them opened DHMO practices, which on occasion I would audit, and they passed with flying colors. They were always under the gun to produce, but when they kept accurate documentation, that resulted in excellent reviews.

The University of Pacific Dental School (UOP) was our next stop. You have to know Sheldon like I do because nothing he does surprises me. We flew to San Francisco with Sheldon leading the way. Andrew and I accompanied him to the car rental counter. Then the fun began. Sheldon was unfamiliar with San Francisco but insisted on renting a large Lincoln. I tried to explain to him that the places we were going to were located on narrow streets with hundreds of parked cars in various positions, not necessarily legal. I explained that a smaller, more maneuverable compact would be a better choice, but not with Sheldon. No way was he going to be seen in a small, innocuous machine. He liked class, and of course he insisted on driving. I tried to tell him that I should drive because I'd been in San Francisco so often, including living there for a year, but he wouldn't listen.

So I rode as copilot. It was a disaster. As a driver, Sheldon was a maniac who liked speed. There is nothing like driving sixty miles per hour swerving in and out down Mission Street with the usual stopped trucks, stop-and-go buses, jaywalkers, and long signals. Our first stop was at the Mission Street Clinic, which has no easy parking. So Sheldon wheeled that big monster into a crowded parking lot with all kinds of derelicts lazing around ogling us in a manner that elicited spinal chills. Of course, we were dressed in business suits, which did not match the neighborhood, and made us all a little nervous. After scaring the hell out of the CDS staff, Sheldon led us back to the parked Lincoln, which was still intact. Then we drove on to the converted whorehouse on Market Street. By this time I was exhausted from constantly directing my boss through town. Even if you know your way around San Francisco, there are always new challenges to the driver.

After our Market Street visit it was now near noon, which was our time to drop off the $163,000 check to the dean of UOP. Negotiating our way to the school again left me a nervous wreck. We finally made it to the school, which is located on a narrow street across from a hospital. Now the time had come to park that big tub. All the spaces on the narrow streets were filled. I told Sheldon about the dental school parking structure and led him through a difficult left turn into the entry, which is located on the side of a street that has a sharp incline. He pulled the Lincoln into the entrance, where we saw a "Full" sign.

After many interesting words from Sheldon, he began a series of fifteen back-and-forth movements of the Lincoln to get it aimed downhill. After several trips around the school, we finally found the entry to the hospital parking structure. We were only forty-five minutes late. The dean accepted our tardiness and donation with graciousness, quite different from the USC experience.

Getting back to the airport in time with no tickets or scrapes was a miracle.

Loma Linda University Dental School was our last stop. There were no volunteers to go with Sheldon except me. I went on one condition--I drive. Sheldon wanted a limo, but he finally acquiesced to let me drive. There were two reasons for his concessions: he had no idea where Loma Linda was, and after San Francisco, he knew I wouldn't let him drive. I owned a modest-model Mercury, but it was new and comfortable. On the drive there, Sheldon was on the cell phone the entire trip. No question about it; he was the consummate workaholic.

Once we arrived, I cautioned Sheldon about his language and his crude jokes. I reminded him that Loma Linda was a Seventh Day Adventist college and that he should afford them a genteel approach.

All went well with the introductions. The dean introduced several of the staff dental instructors, interspersed with some corny humor, and then said, "Let's pray." I was impressed that even Sheldon lowered his head with respect to the Lord. Then luncheon was served, with the main course of vegetable lasagna. (It's important to note here that SDA adherents are generally vegetarians). Of course Sheldon couldn't resist and said, "Well, at least it's kosher." I pretended I didn't know him. Sheldon presented the check and gave a brief speech, thank God, with a minimum of outlandish statistics, and we left for CDS headquarters.

Chapter 18

Experiences with Providers

While I was working for CDS, I made countless visits to many unique facilities that were providers for the CDS DHMO plans. Many of these dentists were not new to me. I had previously recruited them for Den-Cap (DC). Many DHMO providers took all the various competing DHMO plans in order to maximize their patient book of business.

This chapter relates some of my memorable experiences with a few of these providers. I must admit it was a lot of fun mixed in with some pathos.

San Diego Area

All the San Diego offices were necessary to complete the service areas required by the DOC. So I met many dentists who had considerable experience in building successful practices by knowing all the nuances of the capitation business. Many of these offices serviced only DHMO patients, eschewing private patients, and they were financially successful.

The office of Dr. Richard Katz is located in north San Diego in a large strip mall comprised of colonial-style buildings. It was quite nice. He had only the one office, but he was so busy that he employed seventeen hygienists as well as three dentists. Richard, saw a minimal number of patients himself, but he had worked the DHMO programs with such sophistication that the DOC felt justified to routinely keep an eye on him. He was not a popular dentist among his colleagues because of how well he worked the system, which was treating as many patients as possible, performing lots of non-covered optional treatments, and using smooth selling techniques. There were very few complaints from patients about quality. As usual, benefits issues were the main source of grievances. I spent many hours with Sabrina, the very knowledgeable office manager, discussing their techniques. Non-covered benefits seemed to occupy every treatment plan. She was very charming but devious. I would make my points, she would acquiesce, but my next visits merely verified that her acknowledgements were only lip service. Termination of this office was never a consideration by either provider relations or marketing. Richard was too much of a cash cow.

Dr. Jim Kasket apes Richard's style, but he has several offices, including one large facility in a large medical building located under the sprawling freeway interchange of the CA 805 and CA 8 in the San Diego Mission Valley. One of his offices was in the East Chula Vista area, which was managed by his very eccentric hippy-like daughter. It was fun going there because of the anticipation of what appearance she would assume, especially regarding hair and shoes or which gemstone would adorn her bellybutton. Her multicolored coifs never disappointed. Father Jim explained that she had been psychoanalyzed so many times that her shrinks gave up. I admired his obvious love and concerns for his daughter's wellbeing. Each time I went there, she seemed to become calmer and less demonstrative in her appearance, and the patients loved her. I think it was her father's unconditional and ongoing love that helped turn her around.

Jim's office was another challenge for Quality Management because of his wild distortions of the covered benefits. Many patients complained about charges and the office's strange interpretations of the covered benefits. Regardless, Jim was needed. His many offices had huge enrollments and were valuable to the marketing department because of their strategic locations.

Dr. Stewart Tawdry was and still is a constant pain in the neck. The rules mean nothing to him, yet for some reason he is still on the panel of most of the DHMOs. The trouble is that I like the guy. I tell him to his face that he is theoretically breaking many rules, but he merely laughs. He has many contracted dental facilities, from Vista to San Diego. My problem with this guy is that he has never shown any improvement through the years with respect to the quality criteria that are accepted by the industry, but I had never been able to get him terminated. This is because of the pressure exerted by marketing for long provider lists. It is axiomatic that long provider lists offer a much better chance to impress the HR people that our company can guarantee quick access to dental treatment.

At one point I had a meeting with Stewart at 6:00 AM at his Vista office so we could review his various CDS programs. It was my chance to chastise my crazy friend. A dental office is like a tomb at that time in the morning, with no other people there and the missing hiss of the high-speed drills. We went over every plan, reviewing the patient benefits as well as exclusions and limitations of each individual program. It's amazing how many different contracts there are, and how they are all alike, usually with one or two minor differences that are concessions to the vagaries of the HR people. Stewart assured me that he would implement the necessary concessions after meeting with his office managers. For a while he did follow our agreements, but slowly reverted to past habits, which kept me constantly calling him on the carpet. The trouble is that no matter what I said or threatened him with, he went on his merry way. After many years of frustration, we finally had to terminate his contracts. Too bad, he was a cool guy.

I first met Dr. Anthony Garfellow when I was recruiting dentists for the east San Diego area. He was a down-to-earth guy who was not concerned about the threat of lawsuits. He was actively involved in at least five malpractice cases, which apparently did not wear heavily on his conscience. Yet I couldn't help but like him because of his energy and attitude. His office was on a street lined with old eucalyptus trees on buckling streets and the venue for old medical-dental two-story buildings. He was in one of those buildings in a spot on the second floor that was almost invisible. His office was a mass of clutter, but he didn't seem to care. He explained that he was getting ready to move to a new structure on the other side of town, which he owned. The new office was hugely successful and very busy with both DHMO and private patients. He and his wife lived in an apartment just behind the main office building, which also housed three other non-professional rentals.

Unfortunately, Tony ultimately became restricted in his ability to treat patients because of slowly developing Dupuytren's contracture. This is a terrible disease for dentists because it causes a gradual contraction of the tendons in the palm of the hand. It makes it impossible to straighten out the fingers without excruciating pain. So he hired several associates and had his son run the business end of the practice. He limited his activities to oral diagnosis. He subsequently moved again to new facilities, which were more modern and an improvement over his last office. He was very astute with regards to the local real estate, and therefore never sold his buildings. He merely cleaned them up and rented them.

Tony ultimately cleaned up his lawsuits and has maintained a very active and lucrative practice. There were the usual grievances, mostly over benefits.

I have fond memories of Dr. George Steel's office, because through the years he probably was the most screwed-up dentist I ever met. The office was located in Pacific Beach in a building near the beach that he owned. It was a rustic two-story with a subterranean garage. It was never in top shape because George was too busy with divorces and girlfriends. We would have long discussions, but never about dentistry--usually his love life. He couldn't remember how many times he had been married. much less his affairs. George hardly worked and had an efficient associate who did most of the dentistry.

The office was a very weird layout, with a large waiting room that was shared with another dentist who rented space. I received a call one time to help them remove a dead fish from the waiting room aquarium. It was amazing that they would need me to help them, but no one in the office had the stomach for the removal and disposition of the bulbous and homely goldfish. It really wasn't my line either, but I did have to perform our annual review of the facility and was "luckily" present for the piscatorial ceremony. I didn't even have a veterinarian license.

Location kept this office on the plan, and as long as George stayed away, the associate's dentistry was quite adequate.

Dr. Jordan Janowich, or JJ, as we called him, had his office in the second story of a large medical-dental complex toward the west end of the palisades overlooking San Diego Harbor. It was almost hidden because the buildings had been built in the 1960s, were showing signs of wear and tear, and were engulfed in a forest of messy eucalyptus trees. JJ was a panda nut. In 1987, when the San Diego Zoo acquired two giant pandas, Bai Yun and Shi Shi, JJ had gone to the zoo to witness the spectacle of the staging of these two beautiful animals. He became obsessed with pandas, which is demonstrated in his office. Pandas hang from the ceiling and from the bracket tables of the dental units. They sit on every shelf, on top of the filing cabinets, and in the lab. Pandas are everywhere.

JJ was a fair dentist and was well liked by his patients. The office manager, Geraldine, was a gruff, middle-aged woman with a heart of gold (or mold). We got along fabulously. The office itself was a mishmash of narrow halls that led to three dark operating rooms. You had to go through the lab, which was also the lunchroom, to get to JJ's chaotic, private panda-glutted office. We had lots of interesting discussions about the state of present-day dentistry and the pitfalls of the DHMO business. It was almost impossible to evaluate his charting and patient care because he spent more time with his main hobby (besides pandas), sports cars. At my last visit I learned he acquired an absolute cherry Lamborghini red convertible capable of 200 mph. Where JJ got all his money was a mystery. It certainly wasn't from his dental practice; he worked only three days a week. The company kept him on because of his location and lack of grievances.

I had known Dr. David Jermaine of National City since his days of running a small, one-chair office. Things had changed for David. He got a divorce, had a heart attack, remarried, and opened a huge facility in the east side of town. He had become a prolific provider for CDS but had a hard time when it came to completing proper charting of his dental records. So I spent an inordinate amount of time there. My regular contact there was his office manager, who also was his new wife, Rosa. She was a really something. Where David was quiet and genteel, Rosa was a buzz saw. She was a short, plump gal who managed David, not just his office. She raved on about how she wanted David to expand his practice, buy new or old practices, and become a dental dynasty. Just talking to her for any length of time wore me out, but she was fun. What fascinated me about her was her jewelry. She always wore Spanish-style blouses that showed her arms, which I could barely see because of her bracelets, bangles, and an immense diamond-studded wristwatch. Every finger had rings, mostly with huge stones, some precious and others ersatz.

The last I heard about David was that he again was in the hospital with another heart attack. You bet your shirt that there was no pre-nup. Good going, Rosa!

CDS had a few providers in Mexico, since many of our contracts were with companies in San Diego County whose employees lived in Tijuana. Dr. Pedro Estrada was one of them. Pedro's office was unique because of the layout. The entry to the office led into one of the operating rooms. A patient sitting in the dental chair would have to shift his legs in order to afford passage to the hall, which led to the business office and the waiting room. In spite of the ridiculous arrangement of the office, it was well within compliance with our strict criteria. The dentistry was excellent, accompanied by thorough sterilization techniques. The office was spotless. (Many offices charged patients for sterilizing their instruments. I often wondered what would happen if the patient declined the charge and said, "If you use dirty instruments, it's okay with me!")

I was always concerned about parking at the office, but I always found a parking garage protected by a sleeping guard. I always would let out a sigh of relief when I found my car with all its hubcaps and tires intact.

Dr. Pietro Englasis owned a large, modern medical-dental building near the entrance to Tijuana one block from the border checkpoints. Pietro was smooth and very proud of his successful practices, one in Tijuana and the other in Mexicali. He demonstrated his success by always wearing a diamond-studded Rolex wristwatch and two or three huge diamond rings on his well-manicured fingers. I would occasionally meet with him, along with our marketing agent, for lunch in the National City boat marina in California at a very high-end restaurant on his tab. He would always have valet parking for his black Mercedes-Benz convertible. He constantly bragged about how he got around the benefits limitations of our plans, which irritated me no end, but he had a lock on the CDS market because of the lack of providers in the area. Grievances were rare because of his captive audience. He was always looking for additional deals; hence, the requested presence of a marketing rep. And it worked. He was a valuable provider. I could never understand how he was so financially successful when dealing with the very poor who lived in Tijuana.

I never visited the Mexicali office, but I understand it was as nice as the Tijuana facility. Both facilities had the latest and most expensive equipment, which seemed incongruous considering the limited financial resources of Pietro's patients.

So many CDS personnel who worked in the Chula Vista, National City, and San Diego centers lived in Tijuana and commuted across the border daily. Likewise, many dental personnel in the Tijuana offices lived in South San Diego County and commuted to Tijuana. Weird!

Northern California

Dr. Larry Kool operated at least six dental offices in Sears stores in the Bay and Sacramento areas. His business offices were located in rented homes in high-end residential areas. At one time he rented a beautiful home in San Leandro, using it as his headquarters until the neighborhood complained to the police and the homeowner's association. The next time I saw him, he was in a rented home in the Folsom district of Sacramento. This beautiful house had five bedrooms, six baths, and a swimming pool. Larry figured he would last there about another three months before the neighborhood turned on him. I asked his secretary about the finances of their operation. They figured that it was much cheaper to move all their office equipment to newly rented homes. The rents for the houses were much cheaper than office space, and they could live in them too. They were like gypsies.

The quality of their facilities in the Sears stores was very suspect. The waiting rooms looked like Midnight Missions. They had huge booking problems; there were long waits for the patients, who always had all their family with them--crying babies and active toddlers that spelled chaos in the crowded waiting room. All the equipment was old and worn, but they complied with the standards of appropriate barrier protocols. These facilities are no longer on the CDS panel of providers. Larry sold them off and has not practiced dentistry for many years.

The Happy-Smile Office in South San Francisco is not typical of many of the Happy-Smile offices. Happy-Smile is a dental company that owns many large facilities throughout California. This particular office is located in a large shopping mall in the San Francisco peninsula area. When I first saw it, I was amazed by its immense size. To get to it, I had to walk down a long flight of stairs squeezed between two large department stores. It had the look of a car dealership without the cars, having a large open area that contained nothing but a mass of folding chairs, cardboard boxes, old metal file cabinets, and stacks of manila folders containing hundreds of pages and x-rays and held together by rubber bands. In the middle of this room was a business area that was enclosed by a Formica-topped counter. It was the most unprofessional reception room I'd ever seen. The office manager was a pleasant middle-aged woman whose appearance suggested a hard but happy life. She was a gentle, friendly, and very knowledgeable lady. She was a great help during a difficult audit.

The staff consisted of an assortment of dentists performing all the different disciplines of the dental field. The support staff of dental assistants were young women and men dressed in well-worn white dental uniforms. The dental equipment was old but updated and functional.

In spite of the overall appearance of the operating rooms, the facility was acceptable according to CDS standards. Auditing the charts and progress notes was a formidable task because each patient file was approximately two inches thick with what seemed like thousands of loose x-rays. This boded well for me in evaluating the quality of treatment because of the plethora of post-operative x-rays in the files; but the lack of organization in the charts made it difficult and time-consuming to dig out the necessary documentation to ensure an accurate evaluation.

As with most Happy-Smile offices, this office had a huge turnover of dentists. This emphasized one of my concerns with such large offices--patients rarely receive treatment from the same dentist upon subsequent visits. Thus, it is impossible to establish a close doctor-patient relationship.

Most Happy-Smile grievances we received were over benefits. There was a trend of over-diagnosis, which always generated more income for that office and more headaches for us. However, if quality of treatment were an issue, to its credit this practice readily corrected the deficiency. For example: If a crown was deemed ill fitting, the patient was recalled, and the crown re-made without argument or rationalization.

Dr. Theodore Markham, who practiced in Menlo Park, was an older gentleman and a pack rat. He had bought the practice from an old-timer who baked his own porcelain crowns, made his dentures, and cast his gold crowns. He had a very small, triangular-shaped lab that housed his sterilizer and most of the supplies needed to operate his practice. Dr. Markham still had all that old equipment, a porcelain oven, a burnout oven, a casting centrifuge, flasks for dentures, and more stuff piled up and jammed into the corners. It was fun to look at all the old equipment that is no longer used by the profession, but I told him flat out that he needed to get rid of all that junk so that his office could pass the facility audit that our plan required. He smiled and said, "I'm still having fun doing dentistry. Are you going to take that away?"

That question, of course, made me feel like a pariah. I compromised and said, "Of course not, but the next time I come by, which will be approximately twelve months, I hope that you could at least put some shelves up and organize that room." He laughed, and said, "Okay!"

I told his office manager, who happened to be his wife, that if he didn't comply, I would call her and we would rent a Dumpster and get rid of all that stuff.

Dr. and Mrs. Markham were wonderful, and I could see that the patients loved the office and the dentist. I had a chance to speak to many of them in the waiting room while waiting to conduct my exit interview with the dentist. Dr. Markam was obviously a well-respected and beloved dentist in Menlo Park.

My next visit was about a year later, and I was pleasantly surprised at the renovations that had taken place. Neat shelves were installed in the lab, along with a few shallow cabinets. Dr. Markham now had counter space, a new sink, and a modern model trimmer. There were no signs of the old equipment. It looked great. I cancelled the Dumpster.

I visited an office in South San Jose, Fable Dental, which was one of our busiest providers. I called the dentist-owner, Dr. Manfred Fable, the "Gray Fox" because of his long, silvery white locks. He was a very handsome middle-aged man. The office was immense, with general dentistry on one side and specialties on the other. His clientele ranged from the low end to the middle class. The area around his office was eclectic, with some bare-boned abodes to some pretty fancy homes. I spent many hours of deep discussions with this very smart man, who explained the nuances of the DHMO business to me. I thought I knew it all, but found out that I was still learning, even after all the years I had put in and all the offices I'd visited.

Then the cap of the day happened. I'd returned to my hotel and ran into a couple of dentist friends of mine in the lobby. We were talking when all of a sudden I was flat on my back ten feet away near the brochure rack. I'd been hit in the back with a refrigerator! This was a full-sized refrigerator on a dolly that was being pushed through the lobby by a bellman who couldn't see where he was going. I ended up at the emergency room, was prescribed pain medications, and ordered a back brace that I had to wear on the flight home. Nobody in the office believed me. They all accused me of falling off a barstool.

An office in Stockton had two dentists who had separate practices but shared the waiting room. The front desk served both practices. The wives of the dentists worked the front desk. It was obvious from the onset that they hated each other. They didn't speak to each other or look at each other. The awkwardness was laughable.

A solo practice in Fremont had a more awkward atmosphere. The dentist had his first wife running the front desk while his second wife was his chair-side assistant!

While I was in Stockton, I stopped by a pedodontic office and visited with Dr. John Little. I had heard through the grapevine that he was a highly respected dentist who treated kids without general anesthetic. His office was set up with his invention of a dental chair, which was like a physician's examining table. The unit had drawers and attachments that kept all the drills and suctions hidden from view. There was one operating room that had four of the units in a line without separating partitions. He was working on a three-year-old girl, who was slightly sedated with nitrous oxide and a local anesthetic. When he completed his procedure, it took about ten minutes for the child to completely recover. She stayed in the chair until she was alert. She smiled when she jumped off the table and immediately headed for the toy box.

I asked John if he ever used a papoose board. His negative response was accompanied with a long diatribe about such unneeded brutality, which verified my opinion about how to handle kids. Incidentally, he never allowed the mothers in the operating room.

It was de'ja vu all over again when I visited the SmileTech &Vision (STV) office in Modesto. I had visited this practice previously when recruiting offices for DC in the Bay Area. This dentist, Dr. Leon Laufter, taught me many things about the DHMO business that I didn't know. For example, he told me about the existence of the 999 File, which is used by many of the DHMOs. The file is a means of storing enrollees in a list but not assigning them to a provider. This means that they are not on any provider patient list, and thus the provider does not receive capitation until they are assigned. This is contrary to the spirit of capitation and means the dentist is not receiving capitation for a given patient until the patient calls in for an appointment. Simply put, the company is cheating the dentist.

Leon also told me of the shenanigans of STV regarding patients he treated. Once he completed treatment of the patient and placed him on recall, STV stepped in and reassigned the patient to one of its clinics so that the clinics would then receive the capitation instead of the dentist who had done all the work. He finally took them to court and won.

Oddly, I ultimately went to work for STV. The company's reputation in the DHMO field had been sullied by such exploits. Subsequently, it divested itself of the clinics and is now a DHMO, PPO, and indemnity company.

The Los Angeles Area

Dr. John Gould was one of the leaders in the DHMO field and had a large capitation office in Downey. He had one facility on one corner that was pure capitation and on the other corner an office that he called a "private" practice. He practiced general, non-insurance dentistry in this office. The reason I mention him is that he was the most vocal advocate of the DHMO system in the state. He gave seminars on capitation and how to make it profitable throughout California. He mastered the utilization of optional (non-covered) treatment and was an expert at explaining the system to the seminar participants.

However, when I audited his office, I found many deficiencies in charting and diagnosis that seemed to indicate that he had not practiced what he preached. Many of his treatment plans were loaded with "ala carte" dental procedures--procedures that contained extra charges for things that should have been considered integral parts (unbundling) of the treatment. For example, a filling was placed, which was the patient's covered benefit, but there was an extra charge for a "desensitizing" liner under the filling. The liner should be part of the filling. Again, patients must beware and be wary.

Incidentally, the associate dentist who ran John's "private" office across the street committed suicide. The reason for the suicide was never revealed to the public, and the office was never opened again for dentistry, but was rented to a real estate broker.

So Dr. Gould confined his dentistry to DHMOs, and never again ran a private practice. He is still giving expensive seminars.

Foot-in-mouth time occurred with an office in South Los Angeles. I had known this dentist from Den-Cap days. Dr. Homer Hardnose was an African-American dentist. We had become good friends, so when I called his office to make an appointment for an audit, I luckily got Homer himself on the phone. We were having a hard time finding a day that would suit us both because he wanted to be sure to be there when I was there. We finally hit the right time, and I said innocently, "Good boy; that'll work just fine."

Well, when I went there for the audit, he greeted me like I had the plague. I went about my audit, and when I was walking toward the door, Homer beckoned me to come into his private office. He looked me in the eye and said, "Don't you ever call me 'boy' again!" I was flabbergasted and apologized all over the place. It never occurred to me that he was that sensitive and that I had said something to offend him. Homer finally smiled and we renewed our friendship, I hope. I guess that stuff is still alive and well in some people. It never even remotely occurred to me.

◆　　　◆　　　◆

On occasion I was invited to participate in a trade show with the marketing people. At a trade show the company reps set up tables that display the various dental plans that are available, as well as toothbrushes, tubes of toothpaste, dental floss, and many other giveaways for the visitors. The main attraction was that they always got fed. These shows are usually for enrollees in existing dental plans with our company, but they reinforce our interest in the patients' wellbeing. I would go along to answer dental questions and try to act distinguished, since I'm a doctor.

On this particular day the trade show was held at Bell Gardens, located in the southeastern part of LA County. It is also the home of one of the biggest Indian casinos in California. CDS had a contract with all the employees of the casino, including culinary and dealers. The clientele of this casino are mostly Asian; they are gambling fanatics and heavy smokers. You need an axe to cut through the smoke—and the stink—in the casino. Luckily, our trade show was outside.

Things were going along smoothly, with me answering all questions in a distinguished manner. Then came the phone call. The main office called me about a complaint from a patient at one of our Inglewood offices. She complained of cockroaches. The office requested that I leave the show, go over to Inglewood, and check out the cockroaches. So away I went.

Inglewood is about seven miles due west of Bell Gardens. The drive takes you through one of the bleakest areas of South LA. There are miles and miles of unkempt homes, grassless front yards, and the sullen, unemployed gentry that usually bodes unrest and unhappiness. As I was driving along the main east-west thoroughfare, an armada of seven squad cars, sirens blaring, roared past me. After a short time I passed an intersection where the seven police cars formed a semicircle. All hands displayed rifles and drawn pistols and were looking down over the dead body of a large black man in a pool of blood.

I finally arrived at the Inglewood office, which was on the second floor of a medical-dental building. The second floor offices opened onto a balcony, which overlooked a garden area of a few green plants showing a paucity of watering..

Bertie, the office manager, was anxiously awaiting me. She knew me from my many years with Den-Cap. Bertie said, "Dr. Pedersen, I've looked and looked, but I can't find any cockroaches. I can't even find ants. What should I do?"

"Well, you've got me. I'm the master of looking for insects if I do say so myself," I lied.

Bertie and I went through the office and even the front porch area on our hands and knees and found nothing but an occasional piece of lint. The place was spotless. So I told Bertie not to worry, that CDS would send the patient a letter of explanation. If she didn't want to return, we would reassign her, which probably would be best for the office.

Well, there you have it. In one day I was a distinguished doctor, a witness to a killing, and a pest control man. That's true multitasking.

Chapter 19

"Snow Job"

After its settlement with the state regulators, CDS turned its attention to monitoring the centers. This meant that I had to go to an assigned center and spend an entire day reviewing the quality of treatment that was documented in the charting. The regional directors had been reviewing their centers, but they were more interested in production than the quality of the treatment.

It was also essential to keep track of the dentists who were working in the centers. The regional directors often moved dentists from one facility to another for various reasons. Credentialing the new hires was a constant challenge because it was not unusual for either the managing doctors or the regional directors to hire a dentist on the spot because of production pressures and the chronic absenteeism of many of the new graduates. This happened a lot on the weekends, which made it impossible to verify licenses immediately. A lot of these "quick" recruits did not have valid licenses, so there were many Monday terminations. In fact, some of these "dentists" were not actually dentists. There were documented cases of illegal immigrants, especially from Mexico, practicing dentistry in deserted buildings and even garages.

Subsequently, CDS hired and trained dentists to perform audits of the centers supplementing me. By this time CDS had one hundred centers, including orthodontics, well on its way to its goal of one hundred twenty California centers. It was important for me and the other auditors to maintain communications with the regional dental directors, who were more cognizant of the staffing of the centers, so that when we went to a particular center we would not surprise the managing dentist. We were able to review the charts of the dentists who were working in a particular center and evaluate their diagnoses, treatment plans, and quality of treatment.

The regional directors had great leverage over the managing doctors and could exact monetary sanctions against them when they or one of their staff made mistakes, not only in treatment, but also in financial documentation. The managing doctors made a lot of money and were paid a percentage of the center's gross receipts. They were responsible for handling the overhead of the center. A look at the appointment book of a center was beyond comprehension. It was possible for one dentist to have at least three patients scheduled in the first hour. The centers did not have hygienists, so the doctors performed the cleanings and were usually given fifteen minutes for a "thorough" treatment. Most of the dentists in the centers would see around twenty to thirty patients a day.

Every patient received full-mouth x-rays, which were developed and placed on a view-box in the operating room before being examined by the dentist. This has always been a sore spot with me. The policies and procedures of the company clearly state that the dentist examines the patient first and then prescribes the type and number of x-rays needed for a correct diagnosis. The charting indicated that the dentist saw the patient first, but this simply was not true. The same was true for the so-called informed consents that were signed by the patients or their guardians. The dentist was supposed to review the risks and benefits of the treatment with the patient. This never happened. The patients signed the consents before being seen by the dentist. No wonder the patients never understood their treatment.

I thought I had seen almost everything when I encountered a situation with a rebellious Iranian dentist at one of the centers. He was guilty of many cases of over-diagnosis as well as inappropriate treatment. His main quality, however, was his charm. There was no question that he was cool and very likeable. So in my gullibility, I made a serious attempt to rehabilitate him with help of his regional director. We succeeded in getting him a managing dentist job in one of the San Diego centers. For a few months all went well, with no issues emanating from San Diego. Then came the call. He had diagnosed and made an upper fixed bridge replacing the patient's six front teeth. The problem was that the supporting teeth were loose from gum disease. Needless to say, the bridge failed, and another pissed-off patient was created. He was fined by the regional director $4,500 and removed from his managing position. When I went there and confronted him about this case, he replied, "The fine is no problem. I had a great month!" I noticed that he had his spanking new red Porsche parked in the back.

Later he quit the company and opened his own private office kitty-corner across the street from the center. He compounded his offenses by taking some of the dental equipment from the center to set up his new facility. This was a good lesson for me; since then I have been allergic to snow jobs.

Chapter 20

My New Position

It was only a question of time, but finally Glenda resigned and went to work as dental director for another DHMO in Ventura County called General Dental Systems (GDS). She left with aplomb and obvious dislike for Sheldon. Her last statement to Sheldon was, "You're not even a good Jew!"

Jim also left and went to work for Happy-Smile Dental, which was preparing for an audit by the DOC. He was hired for his knowledge of the DOC. Ironically, once he had them cleaned up and passed by the DOC, he was fired. Happy-Smile at that time was known for its abuse of doctors. It was not really "happy." Jim continued with the Air Force, but ultimately retired and went back to Ohio. I haven't heard from him since.

Glenda was replaced with a new dental director, Dr. Takito Kasuka, or "Taki," as we knew him. Taki was a Japanese gentleman who had a wonderful sense of humor, but from the beginning had a terrible fear of Sheldon. I was appointed assistant dental director, replacing Jim. Taki was the master of delegation of work. Quickly, I found that this meant I would do the work of two people. For all practical purposes, I was the dental director, or should have been. In all humility, I think I was a lot smarter than Taki, but maybe not wiser. No matter what, he had a remarkable ability to avoid effort. Who was smarter than whom?

Particularly irritating was my job adjudicating claims. Sheldon would suddenly appear in my office with a smile saying, "Be sure to save me money!" The claims for payment came from specialists and non-panel providers for services that had been authorized by the managing dentists and regional directors. All such claims came across my desk. It was long and painstaking work, especially when under Sheldon's watchful eye. In a way Sheldon had a point. Lots of these claims appeared to be "well upholstered," like a Levitz sofa.

Malpractice

CDS had an in-house counsel, John Kurtz, who was kept busy with a plethora of malpractice lawsuits. In addition, CDS had a legal group in San Francisco that was involved in many of the disputes that were always plaguing the company. I was often consulted to write an opinion, which bolstered my ego.

One very important lesson I learned from reviewing these cases was the necessity of accurate and thorough documentation by the dentist. Accurate medical histories, complete informed consent forms, adequate x-rays, routine cancer screenings, and appropriately signed treatment plans that display all the covered benefits and uncovered options were vital elements of the documentation that protects the dentist. All CDS clinics used the same forms. But often the forms, which were designed to cover all possible situations, were incomplete or illegible. For instance, when I would visit a center to review charts, I noticed that the charts, including the consent forms, were stacked on the front desk counter after the patients were dismissed. They would be completed later in the day! This was and probably still is a problem in all the clinics. How can the documentation be accurate when many hours have lapsed from the actual time of the procedures? They can't be; hence the resultant legal cases.

A good example of the need for proper documentation was the case of an emergency toothache on a weekend. It was the first time the patient had been seen. A routine single x-ray of the painful tooth revealed the need for extraction. The tooth was extracted, post-operative instructions were given, and the patient was dismissed. Two weeks later the patient went to another dentist because he was not impressed by his treatment at the CDS clinic in Pico Rivera. The oral examination of the patient, which included cancer screening, revealed the presence of carcinoma of the tongue. *No cancer screening had been performed at the emergency visit.*

The patient subsequently passed away. A judgment against CDS cost the company $250,000. At every office I visited I always stressed the importance of oral cancer screening. Any patient who sits in the dental chair for even just a few minutes must always be given a thorough cancer screening. If the dentist doesn't do it, you, the patient, should demand it.

Since CDS had so many new grads on the job, they had to handle many issues that should have been handled by more experienced dentists. The problem was that the managing doctors were supposed to monitor carefully the work of their staff dentists. This didn't happen in many cases because of the busyness of the office. Cases of paresthesia, or numbness of the jaws and lips, were common because of amateurish attempts by the new doctors to extract difficult impacted wisdom teeth. Most of the time with such extractions, the sensation of the nerves returns gradually, but there were many cases where sensation did not return. I finally found a neurosurgeon at the University of California School of Medicine in San Francisco who was an expert in the restoration of sensation in the nerves that were damaged. He was expensive, but his fees were miniscule compared with what lawsuits would cost. When Sheldon heard about this, it was one of the few times when he expressed thanks to me—"job well done." Miracle of miracles.

CDS had roving oral surgeons who would schedule appointments at many of the centers. They would usually see patients on a particular scheduled day. The office staff was responsible for the follow-up to the surgical cases because the surgeon would be on his way to another center. One surgeon in particular generated huge monetary numbers but left many post-operative problems that had to be addressed by the general dentists. He had a good set-up--perform the procedure with no post-operative problems to deal with. He left the post-operative follow-ups to the general dentists on staff. He was the fastest operator I'd ever encountered. He was so fast that one of his cases generated a grievance, which came across my desk. He had removed an impacted lower right wisdom tooth. To remove it he had to cut the tooth in half, remove the crown portion of the tooth, and then extract the roots. Post-operatively, the patient was in still in pain. Subsequent x-rays revealed that in his haste the doctor forgot to check the open socket left from the extraction. The crown of the extracted tooth was missed by the post-operative cleanup, and, lo and behold, the missing crown of the tooth had been lodged into the extraction site! Once removed, the piece of extracted tooth caused no further discomfort.

Another surgeon, Dr. Leonora Gildersleeve, consistently left so many patients she treated in considerable post-operative discomfort

Chapter 22

My Years with GDS

I drove out to GDS in December 2001 for orientation and picking up my laptop. GDS was located in Camarillo, a beautiful valley area that still retained a lot of rural color. The company was incredibly generous, buying me a phone, a cell phone, and a fax machine. They paid all my bills that pertained to company business, including mileage, plane tickets, and hotel bills. I immediately started scheduling audit appointments for early January 2002. CDS also had paid my expenses even to the point of giving me an American Express credit card. My card lasted for about a year, but the company terminated it because many of the other users misused theirs. Now, employees must submit their bills for reimbursement.

At the beginning I had to spend several days at the headquarters in order to attend meetings with the DMHC people and familiarize myself with any of the deficiencies that were found from their audits. As it happened, I knew several of the members of the DMHC from the old days when they were part of the DOC. This enabled me to expedite the proceedings and help GDS pass the audit in a timely and profitable fashion. I was off to a good start.

I loved my job. It entailed a lot of driving, which I enjoyed. I visited many offices that I seen before when working for the other companies. It was kind of like "old home week." The most notable feature of visiting GDS providers was their favorable opinions of the company.

There were some exceptions to that last statement. A good example was a dental provider in Palm Springs, Dr. Lester Johnson, whom nobody liked, including his staff. He was a health nut in addition to being obnoxious, and he would often show up at his office in shorts and a sweaty shirt. I asked Phyllis, receptionist, why she had stuck around this character so long even though she obviously could not stand him.

She said, "I live close by and like my little home and my dog. He makes me appreciate what I have when I go home."

My exit interviews with Lester were always confrontational. I would always ask, "Why don't you quit us if you're so unhappy with us? Your charting sucks, your staff doesn't like you, most of your patients don't come back, and I don't like you." I was in this office at least three times during the years, repeating the same diatribe. He would always turn his sweaty back to me and walk away. He is still on the panel.

The GDS office was 107 miles from my home. Driving out there was a long, hard trip, but the trips were few and far between. I would audit providers in the valley areas when I went out there, which made the trips much more productive. GDS held quarterly Peer Review Committee meetings, which I attended. They were very well organized meetings and were usually co-chaired by Glenda and Harold. The meetings were held at dinnertime, so we were fed. (If I'm fed, I'll always make sure to attend.) Since the meetings were held late, on most of the trips out there I would stop by my son Jim's home in Chatsworth, which was at the westernmost edge of the San Fernando Valley. It gave me a chance to see my daughter-in-law and my two granddaughters, and even get some lunch. On occasion I would stop at the Reagan Library on the way down to Camarillo.

Going home after the meetings, which ended around 9:00 PM, was a long night trip. I stayed awake even with a full stomach because in those years CBS Radio carried old radio shows, like *The Lone Ranger*, *The Whistler*, *The Shadow*, and *I Love a Mystery*. They were a little corny, but they kept me interested and made the night drive less boring.

◆　　◆　　◆

Remember my fun with the cockroaches? Well, this time it was ants and a hole in the floor. I was getting ready to leave the house for a trip to Carlsbad when I got an emergency call from Camarillo. There was an urgent call from an irate patient about one of our providers in Del Mar, about twenty-five miles south of Carlsbad. The patient saw ants in the corner of the operating room and complained that the dental equipment was old and decrepit, with a large hole in the floor next to the dental chair. I needed to put it right.

So I drove down to beautiful Del Mar. The office was on the ground floor of a medical-dental building near the racetrack. Once in the office, I met with Charlotte, the office manager, who was obviously chagrined by this turn of events. We went together and canvassed every nook and cranny for ants. No ants. Maybe the patient had "floaters." The hole in the floor turned out to be an aperture for the air lines and the suction lines to the dental unit. The building had a basement, which allowed the dental plumbing to be accessible without having to tear up a slab, which is the standard construction seen today. There was a hole, but so what? We sent a "so what?" letter to the patient.

The lesson here is that the dentist should not leave the patient waiting in the dental chair too long. It gives the patient too much time to sit around, observe, and imagine.

◆　　◆　　◆

I kept running into "stretches," By "stretch" I mean the predisposition of dentists to push the diagnostic envelope for monetary gain. Dr. Dennis Happiston was a dentist I knew from CDS days. He had been a managing dentist at one of the CDS centers. I knew him as a very sensitive guy with high ethics; and the stress associated with the production demands of a CDS center finally got to him. He quit and went out on his own. His office was in the Westminster area of Orange County. Dennis had kept his treatment plans within the standards set by the profession, but his partner, Dr. Douglas Digwell, had a completely different set of criteria. He was the "stretch guy." I got into it with him over the post-operative treatment of extractions. He insisted on placing Gelfoam in the socket after every extraction. Of course, this resulted in an additional charge because such treatment was not a covered benefit under all the plans.

His rationale for using Gelfoam in every extraction made little sense, but he vehemently said he would continue using the material and that I might as well go to the warm place. I knew that the placement of such a sponge in the socket would do nothing but slow down the healing process. It should be used only in cases of excessive bleeding. How he got the patient to buy into this idea was beyond me; but I do know that we had a lot of grievances from his patients complaining of severe post-operative pain. I told him that I would return in six months to evaluate his post-operative protocols and that if he had not changed his ways, I would have to recommend his termination as a provider, even if meant losing my old friend Dennis.

I went back in six months. No change; just a nasty look from a pouting child. I said my goodbyes to my friend and "stretch."

The Merger

Things at GDS went well for about a year and a half. Then things happened. Changes in the company came about through a merger with one of the largest medical insurance companies in the United States. I had not been privy to some of the facts about GDS, such as the fact that it had been on the block since the day I started working for the company. The CEO had been nothing more than a shill who had been hired for working a deal to sell the company. I was really surprised, because he was constantly pushing for perfection, giving the impression that GDS was truly his baby.

The management team of the new company came to GDS headquarters and presented their good qualities to the peons. Always smiling and seemingly understanding, they smoothly explained that we were not getting screwed.

But the inevitable changes occurred: jobs were lost, and new faces appeared in management. Both Glenda and Harold survived for the time being. I was taken off the salaried job and made an independent contractor.

I was doing fine financially as a contractor performing the necessary quality audits. Then the well went dry. All of a sudden the need for audits disappeared. The new company had a huge staff of attorneys who were able to handle anything the DMHC would throw at them. Therefore, the costs of performing quality management were pretty much a millstone that could be defrayed by the legal eagles.

It was as if I were being dishonorably discharged when I had to turn in my laptop. There was no slap across the face with gloves--it was just a quick deep-six. Thus, I bid farewell to Glenda and Harold.

Glenda felt terrible about my demise, but could do nothing on my behalf. She was lucky to keep her own job. She stayed with GDS for a little more than a year, and then was fired on the spot. She sued her former employer for wrongful termination. The suit is still being litigated after many years. They were not kidding about their legal staff.

◆　　◆　　◆

My last hurrah was to audit a new provider in the Carlsbad area. I drove out there and found the new office in a new development that wasn't even in my Thomas Guide. It was located in a large shopping area with all the usual occupants: McDonald's, TGI Fridays, Macy's, Home Depot, Barnes & Noble, and a movie complex. Everything was new, with exterior colors that seemed to be an attempt to copy Mediterranean architecture. It was pretty, but it looked like all the other new shopping centers.

I went to the front desk of the office, with its green marble counter framed by two large aquariums with all sorts of expensive, exotic fish. A stone-faced girl greeted me with a smile that appeared painful. I asked to see the office manager, Hydra, who was sauntering toward the front desk. She smiled and invited me in the back part of the office and sat me in front of a computer. Of course, the office was paperless.

I walked through the office before sitting down at the charting and noticed that it had all the latest equipment that would meet the most stringent requirements of the law. It was nearing lunchtime, and the staff appeared to be having a celebratory lunch for one of the employees, who had announced her pregnancy. The atmosphere was quite noisy, but I managed to dig through the charts on the computer screen. I found an inordinate amount of over-diagnosis, especially in the periodontal (gums) field. Everyone had periodontal disease and needed an expensive periodontal treatment that was not covered by their insurance. I called in Hydra, who was in the midst of the celebration, and reviewed their over-treatment cases. She was quite upset and immediately phoned the owner-dentist, who was not present that particular day. He got on the phone and screamed at me and told me to get out of his office. I told him all I needed was the signature of the office manager. He said, "Get the hell out of my office, and never come back!"

I finished the audit and asked Hydra for her signature. She gave me a look that could kill. It turned out that she was the dentist's wife. I was sufficiently irritated at that point, so I gave her all four barrels. She was very young and not sophisticated, and tears began to flow. I told her she needed a good spanking. With that she finally signed the exit interview paper, and I left, walking through and around the office staff, letting them complete their noon activities. I'm not sure what happened after that, but I assume they dropped off the panel, which would be a good thing. Over-diagnosis to beat the system is unconscionable. It's a shame, because there's plenty of dentistry that needs to be done without padding the bill.

Chapter 23

SmileTech & Vision

So in February of 2004, I was looking again for work. The word was out that SmileTech & Vision (STV) might need someone to help with provider audits. So I looked into who was the dental director there at the time. I found his name, Dr. Perry Moon, and phone number in the CADP directory. I called him and invited him to lunch. My plan was to pick his brains and possibly get some work from him. However, Perry didn't have anything for me at the time. His most interesting comment during our meeting was that the company was female-dominated.

Strangely, just a few days after our lunch together, Perry quit. I didn't know about his leaving until July 2004. When I found out, I immediately called STV about the position to see if was still available. I spoke with a pleasant woman, Erin, who was the vice president of operations. She said the job was still open and that they were interviewing for the position, and she asked me to send in a resume, which I did.

I interviewed with her in early August. She took me around the office to introduce me to the various managers. I told some of my dentist friends, who were familiar with the business, about the interviews. I got the same warning from them all: "Beware of the lady bosses!" They had no doubts as to why Perry quit.

At this time I was financially between a rock and a hard place and needed some sort of assured income. It happened. Erin called to say I got the job and to come to their headquarters and sign papers.

So on September 27, 2004, in spite of the negatives, I became the dental director of STV. I had a beautiful office and met with the staff. They were and still are the greatest people I have worked with through the years, and the most fun.

STV had been functioning without a dental director for almost six months.

Remember, this was the company whose clinic in Walnut Creek I had almost recruited for Den-Cap back in 1987. STV had changed a great deal since then but still had a bad reputation in the industry. It no longer had clinics, but was now strictly a DHMO and PPO. It had been on the verge of bankruptcy in the early part of the new century. The company had a new CEO, who was hired to change its image, make it profitable, and then possibly sell it. Through a series of acquisitions of smaller plans and the dental plans of large medical plans that no longer wanted to deal with the dental portion of the business, STV had become the largest DHMO in California. In addition, STV had acquired offices in Texas and Florida.

My immediate boss was Claudia, an attorney who was in charge of compliance and grievances. She was very pleasant and really knew the law. I was thrown into the position without any formal orientation, just a letter with my job description. My immediate associates, who were indispensable to me, were David and Lara. David was a whiz with the computer, and Lara was an old friend from DC days.

Right off the bat I found that Quality Management was preparing for a DMHC audit and were way behind on provider audits. Luckily, STV had several dental auditors hired as independent contractors who were sanctioned by the CADP to do audits and who could play catch-up once I found which offices needed auditing and how far behind they were in their scheduling. Their computer system was unfamiliar to me, and after a little time there, I found it was unfamiliar to a lot of people.

Meetings, Meetings, Meetings

STV was inundated with meetings. It seemed like the staff had meetings to discuss when they were going to have more meetings. My position was different for me because I was in-house most of the time instead of traveling.

One unique characteristic of this company was its departmental structure. All the necessary organizational groups that are needed for the efficient operation of a DHMO were present, but nobody talked to each other. One department most of the time didn't know what the other was doing. Most meetings consisted of people griping about the other department's shortcomings. It was like running up a down escalator!

Except for my immediate group, the general tenor of the associates was depressive. Talking to most of the people usually would result in complaints about not knowing what's going on. The monthly report from HR, with a long dissertation by the chief operations officer and a picture of his smiling countenance, always extolled the accomplishments of the company in the competitive DHMO world. The huge monetary gains, however, never trickled down to the rest of us.

My job from the beginning was to update the provider audits in order to comply with DHMC standards. Grievances that involved quality of treatment were brought to me for resolution. Early on I made the mistake of thinking like a dentist and evaluating the merits of the grievances from both sides of the issues, the patient and the dentist. On many occasions I would call both the patient and the dentist to make a decision. Claudia sternly reminded me that STV was a benefits company and that my spending the time to converse directly to the parties involved was a "waste of resources." My decisions should always be based on whether the patient received his covered benefits, she said. My determination and opinion of the diagnosis and treatment plans submitted for evaluation had no relevance to the adjudication of the grievance.

While analyzing grievances, if I found that cavities were missed, or if the overall treatment plan was below the standard of care, I would schedule the office for a "focused" review by one of our auditors. Such an audit looked at the particular deficiencies that appeared to be a constant pattern. In some cases, I would go to the offending provider so that the "focused" review would be conducted on a non-punitive basis, literally becoming a form of continuing education. I usually left with a cooperative and supportive colleague. But all these procedures cost money and time and were a drag on the bottom line. Thus, such reviews were frustratingly few and far between.

My Assistants

Once the assigned facility audits were done, it became a big challenge to complete the necessary paperwork and input the data into the computer. Norma, who had been with the company for many years, assisted me in the assigning and adjudication of the submitted audits. Norma was a Christian girl, who was divorced but never got over her ex-husband. She considered herself the most overworked person on the face of the earth. She always complained about her extra work, but she always delivered after my endless prodding.

My job was to complete the final documentation and develop corrective action letters to send to the providers. The paperwork finally became overwhelming, even with Norma giving it her all. So I hired a dentist, Dr. Natalie Parsons, to come in part-time and help with the paperwork. She was a participating STV provider and still practiced part-time with her husband. She helped me in developing case presentations for quarterly Peer Review Committee meetings. This move turned out to be one of my worst choices.

Chapter 24

Committee Work

Every quarter we had a Peer Review Committee meeting, which I conducted. We had the usual mix of committee members—specialists and general dentists, along with Claudia, Liana Thomas of Provider Relations, Lara, and David. Lara acted as the secretary and took the minutes of the meeting. Extreme grievance cases were presented at this meeting. So when final decisions were made, they were based on the input from more than one dentist, which was fairer to the parties involved. I enjoyed these meetings and the camaraderie with my dental peers.

Early on, when I was getting used to the idea of running such meetings, I learned the importance of sticking to the agenda and controlling the time. I found that when any debatable topic came up, all my colleagues became orators, which always screwed up the agenda. Since the company could not afford a gavel, I had to resort to interrupting the speaker and deftly changing to the next subject. One periodontist, when he had an opening, could dominate ad nauseam. Basically, he was constantly pushing the company for referrals to his offices. We couldn't afford him. I later subtly released him from his spot on the committee. I found another willing periodontist, who has been a pleasure to work with, and who has contributed a great deal to the resolution of some of our grievance cases.

At these meetings, Claudia (when she finally got her turn) presented the statistical data to the committee members for their evaluation and discussion. The data consisted of charts that outlined the geographical distribution of the providers, the waiting times for scheduling appointments, the waiting room times, and the times the patient would have to sit in the dental chair before being seen by the dentist. Patient and provider satisfaction surveys were also reviewed. Claudia's reports were always very rosy, but when I carefully reviewed them, they were a stretch. Nobody complained. The participating doctors were paid their honorariums and mileage, were satisfied with the arrangement, and went on their way. I considered most of these reports excellent works of fiction.

The minutes of the Peer Review Committee were always kept on file. They included the resolutions of grievances, discussions of the information supplied by Claudia, and suggested changes to the company's policies and procedures. The Policies and Procedures Manual was continually amended as new problems arose for which the company had no protocol. The manual through the years has become quite large and constructed like a small, one-bedroom house that has been repeatedly remodeled into a six-bedroom monstrosity. They have my signature on many of the policies and procedures that were developed before I was on the company payroll.

Auditor Calibration Meetings

Every quarter I conducted a meeting with our dental auditors at which we would review the Quality Management guidelines to make sure we were all on the same page. Our auditors were assigned offices that were relatively close to their homes. Most of the time at least eight of the nine dentists would show up for the meeting. I would present them with a case, which they were to review. At the end we would compare notes. Of course, the incentive for them to show up was lunch.

Each auditor had his idiosyncrasies when filling out the audit form. Without looking at the signature, I could always tell who did the audit. Each auditor had a pet deficiency, For example, one doctor would look for periodontal compliance; another would emphasize decay diagnosis, etc. But by and large, there was universal agreement, which was the whole idea of these meetings. The auditors performed their reviews on paper. This was a change for me because my former employers always used laptops. But cheap is cheap. When a company is up for sale, the bottom line is the most important selling point. Expenses must be minimized.

The Credentialing Department

The Credentialing Department kept track of all the dentists who performed treatment for STV, making sure that these dentists were *real* doctors with *real* licenses, and not hackers operating out of some back room or garage. Lorraine was the manager of Credentialing and held monthly meetings that included her staff, call-ins from the Florida and Texas managers, and me. We would review the credentialing that had been done for the last month as well as dentists who were being re-credentialed. We referenced a national database to ensure there were no negative entries against the dentists who were being examined. It was my job to review and sign off on each submission. We discussed possible sanctions against dentists who had serious judgments against them. Some of the submissions read like soap operas: The dentist was on drugs or alcohol. The dentist extracted the wrong tooth. The dentist shot his wife. The patient died. In some instances we felt sorry for the dentists, such as those who had a negative against them for failure to completely pay for their student loans. We usually compromised on such cases but always made sure to have the offending dentist's explanation on file.

There was a serious, ongoing problem with communication between the Credentialing Department and Provider Relations. Credentialing always had deadlines, and in order to meet those deadlines, it must have input from Provider Relations, whose representatives were supposed to get all pertinent data from the providers, then report their results to Credentialing in a timely manner. It didn't happen, so Credentialing was always behind. To this day it still hasn't been fixed.

Chapter 25

The Corporate Way

On the second anniversary of my tour of duty with STV, I received a visit from Claudia. I thought, *Great, she is going to talk about my raise.* Wrong. Instead, she said that the company appreciated all the work I had done, but it wanted to cut my time in half.

"Why?" I asked.

"It was a business decision," she answered.

STV wanted to create a national dental director who would travel to Texas and Florida to visit some of the providers there.

"Why can't I do that?" I asked.

"I thought that you might not want to do all that traveling."

"I have no problem with that, but I must always take Mrs. Pedersen with me, which I will pay for myself."

Like all corporations, STV didn't want the encumbrance of a spouse while an employee was performing provider relations and the like. I asked Claudia if she had anybody in mind for that job. "No," she lied. I even queried about the possibility of online conferencing, but she said that was out of the question. Of course, now that is the standard for all their meetings.

I agreed to take the part-time position, which actually has worked out for me quite well, except for the financial challenges that the loss of a larger paycheck created. That forced me to find supplementary sources of income. Any dental consulting for other DHMO companies was unfortunately out because of possible conflicts of interest.

STV hired my former part-time assistant, Dr. Natalie Parsons, as the national dental director. I didn't want to believe that my age or my sex had anything to do with the switch, but the favoritism soon became obvious. She was allowed to do public relations jobs for which I had been turned down repeatedly because they were deemed too expensive.

Ironically, after she became my boss, she never left the state. It was determined that those trips would be too expensive.

Natalie started the job with little or no relevant experience, except for the fact that she had been a provider for STV when she was actively practicing. I had previously audited her office, which was a very good, compliant facility. That's why I had thought of her when I needed help with the audits and the preparations for the Peer Review Committee meetings. Of course, it backfired, resulting in my demotion to a lesser role.

The move from full-time to part-time employee has brought some benefits. It has allowed me to pursue my hobbies, such as playing the piano. It has also given me the time to write this book.

It's taken me a long time to get it, but working in the corporate workplace is not the same as working for myself. The games people play in the corporate environment appear to be a microcosm of the federal government. Management is comprised of "surface" friends. Each is watching out for himself, even to the point of feigned deep consideration. I love it when especially the women work with each other, smiling and sucking up to one another, but when they turn away, oh, the looks! Luckily there's no blood to clean up from the back-stabbings.

The kicker to all this was that my demotion was the result of the buyout of STV by a larger company, Amalgamated Health Care. The cost-cutting methods were obviously a mechanism to make the company more attractive to buy.

So I have accepted the nature of corporate life. It seems to work the same with all large corporations—a good bottom line leads to profitable mergers or acquisitions. I just did my job, tried not to think, and became a corporate robot.

Grievances

Adjudication of grievances was one of the most important functions of Quality Management. Most providers explained STV's policy regarding complaints to their patients. Grievances ranged from quality issues to complaints about the attitude of the office personnel and/or the dentist's interpretation of benefits. Both Natalie and I reviewed the grievances that were considered quality of care. The grievance associates prepared the responses to the grievances and obtained copies of the charts and x-rays from the providers who were involved.

The bulk of grievances were regarding benefits, but aside from those I found two main types of grievance issues: up-selling by the provider and quality of treatment.

The following is a fictional example of a grievance typifying up-selling.

<u>My Analysis</u>: The patient was seen for his routine prophy (cleaning). He was to have his teeth cleaned by a hygienist, who was new to the office. The hygienist commented that the patient had never had periodontal* charting done and should have that done immediately in order to evaluate his periodontal status. She then stated that she would not perform a prophy on him until he had periodontal scaling along with Arestin** treatment. She never did the prophy. The patient also commented that they wanted to charge him for cancer screening.

<u>My Conclusion</u>: The periodontal chart shows minimal periodontal pocketing except for one contact between a second molar and a wisdom tooth. There is no indication that a routine prophy would not suffice. In addition, it is below the standard of care for the dentist not to evaluate the oral cancer status of the patient as part of the covered dental examination. It is recommended that the dentist be counseled about appropriate periodontal diagnosis and treatment and ethical behavior of the hygienist. The patient should be appointed to have a prophy done as well as a thorough cancer screening.

* Periodontal refers to the gum and bone around the teeth. If there is bone loss that can be measured in a chart, then more complex gum treatment must be done. Most plans cover this "extra" treatment, but a lot of the offices offer specialized periodontal packages at extra charges. The problem is many patients sign off on these programs without first thinking it over!

**Arestin is an antibiotic that is administered into the gum around a tooth that appears to have bone loss. It is supposed to knock out the bacteria that cause gum disease. Its use should be limited to isolated areas around the teeth. It effectiveness lasts for approximately three weeks.

The following is a fictional example of a grievance about quality of treatment:

My Analysis: The patient was treated for a full upper denture and a partial lower denture. #26 (the lower right lateral incisor) was extracted prior to completion of the lower partial. There were many documented attempts to get the correct impressions and bite registrations. The results have been unsatisfactory. It is interesting that there was an additional charge for "custom" impression trays.

My Conclusion: The patient should be refunded all charges relating to the dentures, including the extra charge for the custom trays. The trays should be part of the procedure. It is recommended that the treating dentist take a CE course in the fabrication of full dentures. Provider relations should check this office because of the patient's references to their use of auxiliary assistants. It is not appropriate for any assistant to take final impressions.

This latter case also demonstrates what I call "ala carte dentistry." There is a tendency in all the offices to charge for procedures (unbundling) that should be part of the procedure. In the above instance, charging for the impression tray should be included in the fabrication of a denture. It also demonstrates a tendency of many offices to use auxiliary help to perform procedures that should be done by the dentist.

(The problem with full dentures is that the present day dental schools do not stress or teach the techniques for making full dentures. Implants are now the norm. It is unfortunate because a lot of grievances would not exist if the dentists of today were adroit at making full dentures. Lots of patients can't afford implants).

I must emphasize here that it is not just the DHMO dentists who up-sell and un-bundle dental procedures. It is endemic to the *entire* profession. It's just that private practices have to answer to no one regarding the quality or cost of their treatment. Patients can grieve to insurance companies, but such efforts are usually laced with futility.

The patients bear some responsibility here, because unless they have a toothache, there is no reason for them to immediately sign off on a presented treatment plan. They should go home and think about it. If they have doubts, they should seek a second opinion.

The second opinion solution is somewhat tainted nowadays, because of the change in the ethics of the profession. The odds are that it will elicit a criticism of the patient's treatment from the second dentist rather than support. However, a second opinion is still the patient's best shot, along with recommendations of friends, if the first opinion sounds suspicious.

The advantage of the DHMO is that the patients have an avenue to find a positive answer to their dental needs. That avenue is the grievance form. I'll give you more fictional examples of grievances I created and how Quality Management helps patients and in many cases lends support to the diagnosing dentists. After all, there are just as many problem patients as problem dentists.

More Grievance Examples

1. I got a call from a woman I'll call Anita. She worked for a hospital in the accounting department. She said she had sent in a grievance but wanted to forewarn me that she probably had no case. I told her I would look into the grievance and call her back.

It was absolutely amazing. She had gone to one of our providers for an oral examination and cleaning. As usual, the office was very busy. It was a large practice that included specialists. Well, Anita got there, had x-rays taken, waited an hour, and then the dentist appeared. (Notice that the dentist did not see the patient *before* the x-rays). He examined her mouth with lots of "Tsks-tsks!" It turned out that she had periodontal (gum) disease and would need immediate treatment by their periodontist. The periodontist was in the office only once a month. Luckily, he was there on that particular day, and Anita could have treatment immediately, or she would have had to wait a month. So she went in to see this guy, who told her she needed surgery or she would lose most of her teeth. The surgery would cost $4,000, and she agreed! She filled out a Care-Credit application, was accepted, and had the surgery done. As a consequence of the surgery, she was in considerable pain and wouldn't be seen for a month for follow-up evaluation of the treatment.

The irony to all this is that I had a chance to review her x-rays that were submitted with the grievance documentation. She had a perfect mouth. She had a little bone loss at the back of her second molars, which was the result of her wisdom teeth extractions. I called her and said, "I think you know it, but you've been had." She said, "Yep, I got a $4,000 lesson. I feel real stupid because I'm in the business and know better. But the pressure of the sell was just too much for me to decline."

There was nothing our department could do for her. She didn't even get continuing education credits for her four grand.

To repeat: The patients bear some responsibility here, because unless they have a toothache, there is no reason for them to immediately sign off on a presented treatment plan. Go home and think about it!! And, if there is doubt, seek a second opinion.

2. I received a letter directly from a patient, Herman, instead of a grievance form. Here is an example of the up-sell. Herman went to a large office for a cleaning, x-rays, and exam. He had an upper removable partial denture replacing one of his front teeth and two molars in the back. He had had the partial for a long time, and it was wearing out. Instead of diagnosing a new partial, the dentist went on a long diatribe about the benefits of fixed bridgework. Of course, fixed bridgework was much more expensive and included cutting down of the teeth on both sides of the spaces. Herman just wanted a new partial.

Then the dentist came up with a beaut: "If we make you a partial, you will have to take it out when you eat, and you will only be able to chew soft things." Herman responded impatiently, "But I can eat anything with this ill-fitting partial I have now. Why, would I have to change with yours?"

Herman commented in his letter that even the staff members shrugged their heads when they heard that one. He never did get an answer. He did get the dentist to make his partial, but the quality was poor.

I recommended a second opinion dentist, and STV would have the original treating dentist refund Herman's money. I haven't heard from Herman since.

Chapter 26

Why Patients Pay More Than Necessary

There are thousands of general dentists and specialists practicing in California. As mentioned before, most general dentists have PPO arrangements with many insurance plans. There are also thousands of general dentists who are on DHMO panels. The advantage of the DHMO over the PPO is the cost to the patient. PPO's are always more expensive and are not regulated by the Department of Managed Health Care. Therefore, the PPO dentist's who are not on a DHMO panel do not have to submit to Quality Management audits. One patient protection is not present.

In any case, the cost of doing dentistry nowadays is incredibly high. The cost of going to dental school is in most cases subsidized by student loans from the federal government. Thus, before a graduate even picks up a drill for the first time, he is in the hole usually well over $150,000.

A DHMO is one way a new dentist can get a ready-made list of patients without waiting for the first word-of-mouth referral. Most dentists advertise in magazines, telephone directories, newspapers, and even tracts left on doorsteps or under the windshield wipers of parked cars.

If the dentist has a small staff of assistants, he must incur the cost of workmen's compensation insurance for each member. The rent, the maintenance of equipment, the laboratory bills, the student loan, the equipment finance payments, the malpractice insurance, and various types of required licensing smother the enthusiasm of the new grad. Hence, the "unbundling" of dental procedures and the creation of inventive procedures that are considered elective and therefore not covered benefits. "Unbundling" means itemizing several steps in a procedure separately instead of one inclusive treatment. For example, a crown with a build-up is really one procedure, but is charged separately as a crown and a build-up. Again, I call this "ala-carte" dentistry. This always raises the fee for the procedure.

One thing going for the dentist is the present-day fixation among all ages on appearance. Patients love those white pearls that jump out over the lips exposing glistening white beauty. God forbid that you should see metal. Old, unsightly silver amalgams have got to go and be replaced with tooth-colored restorations. And the gums. Heavens, you need irrigation! You need medications! You need an electric toothbrush! You must have this latest bleaching kit!

Now the trend is toward large practices that are staffed by dentists and specialists who perform all possible dental disciplines, except hospital dentistry. This type of setup encourages in-house specialty referrals and relieves the general dentist of performing procedures that might not be his forte. One of the major disadvantages of such arrangements is that the patients rarely have the same dentist following their case. Thus, the concept of a personal doctor-patient relationship is becoming history.

These large practices have huge staffs of chair-side personnel, sterilization specialists, licensed x-ray technicians, and hygienists. They also have office managers and their assistants who handle the appointments and the financial aspects of the diagnosed treatment plans. The financial people are usually well dressed and smooth. They handle the contracting for treatment. Since most of these offices are "paperless," one naïve patient can get into enormous debt at the snap of the finger simply by placing his signature on the glass grid. When reviewing the documentation stored in the computer, one gets a sense of discomfort looking at the different consent forms, which have digital signatures that look like they have been scanned. It should be a basic assumption that honesty prevails, but there is no question that these new systems could be used to create "fictional" or altered charts that are fraught with creative allegories. The following short stories illustrate the dilemmas patients face when deciding what dental treatment will be best for them:

Naïve Nick

Nick Romeo was just celebrating his thirty-sixth birthday at his parents' house. Most of his family was at the party, including his beautiful wife of eleven years, Eleanor, and their two sons, Nick Jr. and Michael. Nick's two younger brothers and a sister joined in the festivities. The family had finished dinner and Nick's mother, Maria Romeo, started cutting the cake, while his dad, Tommy, conducted the family choir singing "Happy Birthday, Nick." They were terrible but happy and loud.

Nick started to blow out the thirty-six candles and with one powerful gust, out flew an old amalgam filling right in the middle of the *p*'s in *Happy*. His happy birthday smile turned into a grimace. It was strange that it didn't hurt, but it sure left an immense hole in his lower jaw. After the initial shock, the family witnesses recovered from their gasps of surprise and returned to their festive moods. It actually was funny, and Nick was asked if he had made a wish. His sullen look turned into a smile. He said, "I always wish that I don't spit on the cake, but this was ridiculous! Now my wish is that I find a good dentist. It's been three years."

Eleanor had Nick open his mouth wide so she could get a look at the disaster. She said, "It looks like a hole the size of a BB, so it probably feels worse than it actually is."

Nick's birthday had been on a Saturday; it's almost a given that these things happen on weekends or holidays. Since he wasn't hurting, Nick decided not to worry about it until Monday morning. His company had just signed a contract with a DHMO, "Mandible Masters, Inc.," and he knew he would have to call them and find a provider dentist.

Nick worked as the foreman of a computer chip company called Geeketics, Inc., a computer chip foundry that employed about two hundred skilled people. Part of his employee package was a medical program that included an arrangement with Mandible Masters for the dental portion of his benefits. It was a cafeteria plan, which meant that part of the benefits premiums were paid by the employees and part by the employer. The main benefit of the plan was that the premiums were deducted from their salaries pre-tax, thus reducing their salary tax base.

Before he went to work Monday morning, Nick was at the telephone with his benefits packet and phone numbers in hand. He called the phone number of Mandible Masters, which was using a mechanical answering machine that offered him the usual options. "Press 1 for English. ... The following menu will give you a list of numbers. Please pick the one that best suits your needs." Three seemed to be the one, which was "select a provider." After pressing 3, he was instructed to put in the last four digits of his Social Security number, followed by his zip code.

Nick sighed and asked himself, "Will I ever get a human voice?" Just then, after fifteen minutes, the machine asked if he would like to speak to an associate. All he had to do was to press 0 and he was on his way. He pressed 0. A high-pitched voice answered and said, "This is Indira. May I help you?"

Nick answered, "Yes. My name is Nick Romeo, and I'm a new member of your dental program and want to choose a dentist in my area because I've lost a filling. And by the way, where are you located?"

Indira cackled, "Our call center is here in Bombay, and would you please repeat your zip code and your ID number?" Nick repeated the necessary information.

"Give me a few minutes while I look you up. I'll put you on hold if you don't mind," Indira said. Nick sat patiently listening to the latest atonal hip-hop music. Indira came back on the line, "Thank you for waiting. I've looked up your plan, which is HFS223. I've located a dentist within three miles of your home. He is Dr. Mohammed Molar." She then gave him the address and phone number. "If you have any problems about understanding your benefits, please call our Customer Service Phone Line, or you can also obtain most of your needed information from our Web site, www.mandible.chu."

Nick immediately called the new dentist. He got an answering machine, which stated the office hours. He had called at 8:30 AM and found that the office hours started at 9:00. Nick sat at the kitchen table and poured himself another cup of coffee. By now his tongue was almost raw from fooling around with the rough spot on his tooth.

At 9:10 Nick made the call. "Dr. Molar's office, this is Margarita. May I help you?"

Nick said, "Yes. I have been referred to your office by my dental HMO, Mandible Masters. I lost a filling and need an appointment as soon as possible."

Margarita excused herself and put Nick on hold. (More atonal music playing.) "Sorry for the delay," she said. "We are so heavily booked we won't be able to see you for five weeks."

"What am I supposed to do? I have a hole in my tooth. I have a benefits plan that lists your office as a provider. Do I need to call the company back and find out how my plan guarantees dental treatment and an appointment in a reasonable length of time?" Nick asked.

Margarita responded, "We do have a lot of last-minute cancellations. I'll put you at the top of the list."

It was almost 10:00 AM and Nick thought, *Okay, I'll give it a few days. But if I don't get a call back soon, I'll have to call that stupid answering machine at Mandible Masters.* Nick did not realize that Dr. Molar's facility as a provider for a DHMO was in violation of the guidelines of the Department of Managed Health Care, which described wait times before, during, and after dental treatments.

Nick, however, was in luck because Margarita called the next day and booked him for 10:00 AM the next Wednesday. Of course, he had to schedule his time off from work. He promised the office he would be out only about two hours. His time away from work was critical for his job at Geeketics.

Wednesday came and Nick arrived at the dental office fifteen minutes early. The office was on the third floor in a large medical-dental building near the hospital. The waiting room was already jammed with what appeared to be entire families, with their children, the little dolls, running around and raising all kinds of hell. There was a wall-mounted television set that was showing DVDs of the various dental disasters that plague the human race. Nick approached the marble-trimmed front desk smiling and asked for Margarita. According to the receptionist, Margarita did not come in on Wednesdays until 1:00 PM., but she could take care of him. He was presented with a clipboard and a ballpoint pen and asked to fill out the medical history, the dental history, the HIPPA form, the dental materials acknowledgement form, the consent form, and an arbitration form. Nick did the best he could with the forms and then asked how long it would be before he would see the dentist. It was already 10:30, and all that he had at this time was writer's cramp. Another assistant called his name and took him into the x-ray room.

Nick asked, "Should I have x-rays now? I haven't seen the dentist. How do you know what x-rays are needed?"

The assistant answered, "It's our office policy to always take eighteen x-rays of new patients. The doctor then looks at the x-rays and decides what treatment you need."

"But I only came in to get my filling that fell out replaced," Nick said, doing the best he could to control himself. He finally gave in and let her take the x-rays. Once she was done, she shuttled Nick back to the waiting room.

It was getting close to noon, and Nick was really getting antsy. He went to the front desk for the tenth time and asked when he was going to be seen. The front desk girl smiled and said, "Dr. Molar is a little behind, but you're next!" Nick then asked if he could use their phone to call his company because it was well beyond the time he had promised his boss that he would be gone. Luckily, his boss was understanding and told him not to worry about coming back that day. It turned out that Dr. Molar was also his boss's dentist. Apparently he was used to the long waits.

Finally, at 12:40 PM, a smiling dental assistant named Marlene called for Nick and took him into one of the operating rooms, sat him in the dental chair, put a bib on his chest, and laid the chair back to a semi-sitting position. The equipment appeared to be the latest, with a large, wall-mounted TV screen running the dental DVDs that he'd been watching the last several hours. She left the room; still no doctor. Nick could hear the whirr of the high-speed dental drills going. He didn't know if that was Dr. Molar or one of his assistants working. He could smell the aromas of lunch emanating from one of the back rooms.

At 12:50 in strode Dr. Molar. He was a short, stocky, bearded guy wearing a white doctor's coat with open lapels that displayed a neat collar and a really ugly tie. Dr. Molar smiled and said, "I'm sorry to be a little late, but we have had a really busy morning with several emergencies. Well, let's see what's going on."

Nick gulped and said, "Dr. Molar, I really came in just to get my tooth fixed where I lost a small silver filling."

Dr. Molar put on rubber gloves, picked up a mouth mirror and explorer, and asked Nick to open wide while he checked his mouth. The assistant then turned on a small television screen that was mounted on the bracket table of the unit, which also housed three drills connected to long hoses that hung down below the TV mounting. The setup was quite impressive. There in full view were the eighteen x-rays of Nick's mouth. They revealed that he had had his wisdom teeth extracted but had all the rest of his teeth.

Dr. Molar carefully probed his teeth and called off a variety of conditions, which the assistant jotted down. The dentist then left the room. At this point the assistant said, "It is our practice to use the latest technical equipment to examine all your oral structures to screen them for possible cancerous lesions. This procedure is not covered by your plan, so there would be a charge of $150, but it guarantees peace of mind."

Nick commented, "Gee, that's a lot of money and is really out of my league. All my other dentists always checked me for cancer and felt my throat and neck, which I noticed Dr. Molar didn't do. Can't he just check me the old-fashioned way?"

"Well," the assistant said, "if you decline this special examination, you'll need to sign here on this form."

As the assistant left the room, she said, "The office manager will come by in a few moments and go over Dr. Molar's treatment plan with you. She'll explain your benefits, options, and charges."

"But, can't I just get my cavity filled today?"

"That would be up to the office manager and Dr. Molar."

Enter the office manager, a well-dressed, tall blond woman with reading glasses hanging from her neck and a clipboard and pen in hand. "Good afternoon, Mr. Romeo. I'm Heather, Dr. Molar's office manager," she said smiling. All Nick remembered was that she smelled good. She continued, "Dr. Molar has gone over your treatment plan with me, and I'm here to explain to you the treatment you need to restore your mouth to excellent health. We have entered your plan in the computer, and I'll bring it up on the screen here on the dental unit and review it with you."

Heather then started her pitch. "Your chief complaint was the loss of a filling in tooth number nineteen, the lower left first molar. It has a large amalgam filling, part of which is now missing. Dr. Molar notes that the correct restoration for that tooth is a full crown. Your plan has a co-payment of $100 for a porcelain-fused-metal crown. However, the metal in this crown is a nickel-chrome alloy, which is very difficult to fit to the tooth. The better option is a crown that uses noble metal, but there is an additional charge of $250. And for an additional $250, a porcelain margin can be fabricated so that no metal shows."

"Does metal showing on a lower back tooth make any difference to the fit of the crown?" Nick asked.

"Most patients nowadays do not like to show any metal," Heather replied.

"Can't Dr. Molar just patch the existing filling? What would that cost me?"

"I'm not sure because Dr. Molar did not consider that option because of the age of the old filling," she explained. "We'll go back to that in a minute because Dr. Molar has also found other problems, mostly about the condition of your gums. Before he can fix your tooth, he needs to treat your gums. When he was probing your teeth, he found that you had a lot of deep plaque in pockets around your teeth, which requires deep scaling and Arestin treatment after irrigation. Your plan has a co-payment of $35 per quadrant for the deep scaling. But the Arestin treatments, which take in seven teeth, are not covered and cost $165 per tooth. It is also important that your gum treatments are enhanced by irrigation of the gum pockets with an antiseptic solution prior to the Arestin treatments. The irrigation is an additional $300."

Nick was pretty good at math and said, "Wow, that adds up to $2,095. That's a lot of money for walking in here to get a small repair of my molar."

"But Mr. Romeo, we're interested in your complete dental health, and Dr. Molar wants what is best for you. Remember, you haven't seen a dentist for over three years! If you agree to our treatment plan, we'll perform the cancer screening program at no charge, which is a savings of $150."

Nick knew he couldn't afford all this work and said so. Heather, of course, then came up with a solution. "We have an arrangement with a credit company, who will loan you the money immediately without a complicated authorization form. Your signature would immediately give you the wherewithal to get your mouth restored to excellent dental health."

By now Iit was almost 4:00 PM. Nick's bottom was getting numb, as well as his brain. This pressure sell was almost too much for him. His tooth wasn't fixed. He had seen Dr. Molar only once. Heather's demeanor was powerful. Her apparent dedication to getting him on the road to dental health dimmed his ability to accurately evaluate his true dental needs.

You won't believe this, but Nick Romeo caved in, signed the agreement to the treatment plan, and signed the loan application with Usurious Credit, Inc.! The die was cast!

Poor Nick left the office with an appointment in a week to start his treatments and headed for home. He was trying to think of how he was going to explain this to Eleanor. He broke out in a cold sweat when he remembered her comment about how small the cavity in the tooth was. How is he going to explain $2,095 for that small hole?

It was 6:00 PM by the time he got home. Dinner was almost ready, and Eleanor greeted him as always with a big smile and a big kiss. "Honey, how was your trip to the dentist? You're sure late." Nick sat down after pouring himself a drink and told his story.

"Two thousand dollars? How are we going to pay for this?" Eleanor cried.

"Shouldn't you have thought this out before accepting such an outlandish program? You big dope! Your tooth didn't even hurt!"

She sighed. "What's done is done. Let's eat."

◆　　　◆　　　◆

A sweaty, very uncomfortable Nick arrived at the dental office right at the appointed hour. Oddly, he had to wait only a few minutes before being shown into the operating room by Margarita. In walked Dr. Molar, wearing a mask and glasses. He then pulled on rubber gloves. Margarita placed the x-rays on the arm of the bracket table, and Dr. Molar mumbled a few words to her and turned to Nick.

Nick was laid back in the chair so that his feet were actually above his head. A dental bib was placed with a chain around his neck. He asked, "Dr. Molar, is it possible that you could just patch up my amalgam filling, which I understand is a covered benefit at no charge, clean my teeth, which is also at no charge, and release me from the rest of the treatment until later?"

Dr. Molar's glasses fogged up, and Nick noticed that what little of his face he could see had turned a beautiful crimson red. "Mr. Romeo, I have spent considerable time and energy outlining your dental treatment. I would hate to see my efforts go to waste because of fees," he fumed.

"Dr. Molar, you didn't answer my question. Should I maybe go get a second opinion?"

Dr. Molar was apoplectic at this point. He threw his mouth mirror and explorer down on the bracket table and stormed out of the room. Nick tore off his bib and was trying to get out of the chair. It was hard because the chair was laid back so far. Margarita came over and helped him out. She was obviously upset by this turn of events.

Nick shouted, "I want my account with Usurious Credit canceled! I want out of here! This guy's money happy! You're all money happy!" He staggered through the waiting room and out the front door toward the elevator with Margarita in fast pursuit. She grabbed him by the arm while he was pushing the down button and said, "Please, Mr. Romeo, reconsider the situation. I'm sure that we can make arrangements that will please you and renew your confidence in Dr. Molar."

"No way! That guy's a nut!" Nick answered as the elevator door opened. "I'm going to call my carrier and get another dentist, hopefully an honest one."

Nick called Eleanor from work and told her what had happened with the dentist. She was incredulous and asked, "Are you sure you didn't chicken out?"

"No, no," her husband said. "He went bananas when I asked him again if he would just repair the existing filling. He stomped out of the room after throwing his instruments. Actually, he scared the hell out of me! Honey, would you mind calling Mandible Masters for me and see if they would assign me to another provider?"

"I'd love to," Eleanor said. "Maybe I'll get it right! I'll see you at dinner and let you know what happened."

Nick breathed a sigh of relief. He was afraid of all the crap he might have to go through to change providers with such a large company.

Nick came home from work that evening and was greeted by Eleanor with a smile and a cold martini. "Well, I talked to Mandible Masters and they are moving you to another provider," she said. "I then looked up Usurious Credit and called them to find out if your application had gone through. They said yes. They had received it electronically while you were in the chair. I asked them if it were possible to cancel it, and they could not unless Dr. Molar signed off on it. According to Usurious, you have ten days to close that account. I think I'll handle Dr. Molar for you because of your temper and his. But you now a have a new dentist, Dr. Gin Nguyen, who will see you as soon as you make an appointment. He's apparently not very busy, so you shouldn't have to wait very long."

◆   ◆   ◆

Dr. Gin's office was located in a small, one-story medical-dental building that housed twelve offices, mostly medical and one medical laboratory. Nick walked into the small waiting room, which contained six black lacquered wood chairs with silk cushions. In the background Asian music emanated from two square speakers suspended from the ceiling in the corners of the room. There was an aroma of incense.

God, I'm in Vietnam, Nick thought. There were no waiting patients.

Dr. Gin's office manager, Thuy, was a slight, bird-like Vietnamese woman with a pleasant smile and a contrite attitude. *Wow, what a difference from Molar's madhouse*, Nick observed.

The office was of a shotgun design with a long hall that extended to a rear exit. There were four operating areas separated by pre-built modular cabinets. The dental units were approximately twenty years old. In spite of the somewhat cluttered appearance, the equipment seemed to be maintained appropriately. Thuy set the x-ray copies on a cabinet near the unit. They were digital, so a view box was not necessary. *Thanks, Eleanor*, Nick thought. She had managed to get copies from Molar's office for a fee of $25, which is a standard fee.

In walked Dr. Gin, a neatly dressed small man with dark-rimmed glasses that almost covered his face. He resembled a white-clad lemur. He announced himself and picked up the x-ray copies. Nick told him about his experiences at Dr. Molar's and asked about the need for so much work. Dr. Gin checked Nick's mouth and then laughed. He commented that Nick's mouth was in very good shape. He needed a cleaning and a repair of the broken amalgam—all the treatment was at a zero co-payment.

There was no need for anesthetic. The cleaning, polishing, and the repair of the filling took about forty-five minutes. Then Nick was on his way, with a smooth, repaired tooth.

When Nick got home that evening, Eleanor greeted him with good news from Usurious. She showed him the form faxed to them that he needed to sign and date to close the account.

This episode taught Nick a good lesson. Dental-wise he was no longer naïve. It's too bad that one has to go through such a nightmare, but ethics seem to be missing in many dental professionals. But guys like Dr. Gin Nguyen still carry the flag of professional honor and honesty.

Junior's Story

"Momma! Momma! Momma!" cried Junior. "There's blood on my pillow!" Hannah, a single mom, came rushing into Junior's bedroom and found her eleven-year-old son sitting on the edge of his bed bellowing like a dying moose. Blood was all over the sheets and blankets and freely running out of the corners of his mouth.

"Oh, my God!" exclaimed Hannah. "What happened?"

"Momma, I'm bleeding out of my mouth," he sobbed. "My tooth, my tooth is all squishy and feels weird."

It was 7:00 AM, but Hannah decided to place an emergency call to her dentist, Dr. Chargem Wisdom. She got the answering machine, which gave her the option of leaving a message or his pager number. She opted for the pager and dialed the number.

Meanwhile, Junior's bleeding had lessened, and Hannah looked in his mouth, which was filled with blood. She could see a large swollen area and a white molar tooth seemingly floating in the red sea. It looked painful. Junior had quieted down to an idling whimper, so Hannah relaxed a little waiting for the phone.

Dr. Wisdom was on the panel of her DHMO, so Hannah was used to slow responses and delays. However, to her surprise, Dr. Wisdom called back at 7:30.

"Good morning, Hannah," purred Dr. Wisdom. "What's the problem?"

"Oh, Doctor, Junior is hemorrhaging from his mouth. The inside is bloody and swollen. He's crying with pain. Please, can you see him this morning?"

"I'll see you at the office at 9:00. But right now I'll call your pharmacy and prescribe penicillin for the infection. Give him two of the pills immediately before you come in. Two baby aspirin with a lot of water will also help."

The timing was just about right. Hannah got Junior cleaned up and dressed, quickly washed her hands and face, and threw on a warm-up outfit, not bothering with makeup. Then they went to the pharmacy where Hannah had been a regular even before Junior came along. The pharmacist, George Dram, looked at Hannah quizzically and asked, "Has the doctor looked at Junior?"

"No, but he wanted Junior to have two of the pills before we got to the office," she answered. George's frown prompted Hannah to ask, "George, what's wrong? Is there something I don't know?"

"Well, it's unusual for a doctor to prescribe over the phone without first seeing the patient. Nowadays there is a big push by the medical profession to restrain frivolous prescriptions of antibiotics. Patients will build up resistances to them, and so when they are really needed, they don't work. So, please ask Dr. Wisdom about his reasoning."

"Thanks, George, I'll hold off on the pills until after we see him," she said with an understanding smile. Hannah was one smart lady.

So Hannah and Junior retired to the family SUV and headed for Dr. Wisdom's office. Junior was quiet, but appeared very nervous. She parked the large vehicle in the parking structure of the professional building that was home to Dr. Wisdom. It was a large, modern three-story structure with lots of spun aluminum trim and glass and an impressive lobby. Dr. Wisdom's office was on the first floor, just around the corner from the elevators. The office was open even though it was only 8:45 AM. Hannah was impressed. *Wow, they're really on the ball. It's neat that they would get here early just for us,* she thought.

They sat down on two of the elegant, modern overstuffed chairs. Junior liked the waiting room because he could watch the fish in the large custom aquarium set in a large custom mahogany cabinet. The piped-in music was playing, but nobody was behind the front desk. Where was everybody? Junior was getting restless. At least his bleeding had ceased, but the quiet was very hard on an eleven-year-old.

It was 9:05 so Hannah got up and went to the opening to the appointment desk. Just then an elderly lady opened the front door, smiled at Hannah and Junior, and took a seat facing them. Finally from behind the half-wall that separated the appointment desk from the business office appeared Dr. Wisdom's office manager, Gertie. She smiled and said, "Good morning, Mrs. Jones. Oh! Hello, Hannah. Did you have an appointment today? I don't have you in the appointment book."

Hannah answered her question with a question. "Didn't Dr. Wisdom let you know about Junior? I called him early this morning because Junior was bleeding from his mouth, and he prescribed antibiotics and pain pills and told me he'd see us this morning at 9:00. I gave him the pain pills, but held off on the penicillin at the suggestion of my pharmacist."

"Dr. Wisdom is delayed, he but should be here any minute," said a slightly befuddled Gertie. "Hannah, I'll pull Junior's chart and x-rays for the doctor. He should be here any minute.

"Mrs. Jones, I'll seat you now in room one," Gertie continued. To Hannah she added, "We'll take Junior back to room two once I find his file."

Just after Gertie had seated Junior in the chair and sat Hannah on a short operating stool in the room, the rear door of the office opened and in walked Dr. Wisdom. He rushed by the doors to the operating rooms, being careful not to look at the patiently waiting patients, and went into his private office, shutting the fogged glass door.

Gertie followed the doctor into his office. Hannah could hear the muffled tones of an anxious conversation. Dr. Wisdom came out and went immediately into room one to see Mrs. Jones. Gertie went to room two and explained to Hannah that the doctor would see them in a few minutes. Junior was by now squirming uncomfortably in the dental chair. Gertie turned on the corner-mounted television, which was showing the usual dental demonstrations of the home care procedures that ensure good dental health and countless before and after pictures.

"Gee, I wish they had cartoons," whispered Junior.

It was getting close to 10:00 when the doctor ceremoniously entered the room. He warmly greeted Hannah and smiled compassionately at poor Junior, who was by now close to tears. He went to a cabinet in the corner of the room and pulled out a pair of latex gloves and deftly snapped them on his large hands. He wore a white gown with long sleeves that fit snuggly to his wrists with expandable elastic cuffs. He donned a pair of large glasses and went to Junior, who was semi-prone in the dental chair. "How are you doing, Junior?" he asked with a smile. Hannah tried to say something, but Dr. Wisdom raised his hand, signaling for her to be quiet. Hannah leaned back onto her stool and shut up.

Junior couldn't tell if the doctor was smiling because of the mask, but his approach was gentle and reassuring. So Junior opened his mouth as wide as he could. He could hear a few "tsks-tsks" coming from the dentist as he poked around his mouth. Dr. Wisdom turned around and took off his mask and spoke quietly to Hannah.

"Junior's got a large abscessed area in the upper left molar region. The tooth will have to be extracted. I recommend that he be referred to a children's dentist for its removal. It'll be less traumatic, and they'll give him a little nitrous oxide gas, so there'll be no pain. I'm glad he got the antibiotics. That will help the infection clear up quickly with minimal post-operative discomfort. When he's more relaxed, they'll be able to get an x-ray to ensure its complete removal. Gertie will call the pedodontist and arrange an appointment as soon as possible. This type of referral is not covered by your plan, but the charges will be minimal."

Hannah was near tears and forgot to ask about the need for antibiotics. She still had not given any to Junior, though his swelling seemed to be much less even now.

Gertie appeared and said, "I've contacted Dr. Dora's office. They'll see Junior tomorrow morning at 10:30. Be sure he has nothing to eat before his appointment. And be prepared to pay them at the appointment. Their usual charge for such a procedure is around $500 including the anesthesia."

Hannah thanked them and left with Junior in hand. She had a strange feeling that things went too easily, and with Junior's swelling getting smaller, she decided to gamble and not give Junior the medications.

Hannah went straight home and put Junior to bed after giving him a drink of water. Junior was hungry and much calmer, so Momma got him a bowl of Jell-O. She brought him up a tray with more water and the Jell-O so he could get some fluid as well as sustenance. She turned on his television and felt his forehead. He seemed to have no fever. Hannah relaxed and definitely decided to lay off the antibiotics.

Hannah had a fitful night, waking up every hour, turning on her nightstand light, sneaking quietly into Junior's room, feeling his forehead, and returning to bed with a relieved sigh.

"Momma! Momma! Momma!" cried Junior. Hannah jumped out of bed with a start and rushed to his room. Junior was sitting on the side of his bed smiling. "Look, Momma! It looks like a piece of tooth."

"Momma, I feel good!" Junior showed his mother a wrinkled white piece of tooth with sharp edges. "Momma, No more pain."

Hannah asked Junior to open his mouth wide so she could look in. She saw a hole in his gum with a white point showing through the spongy red tissue. Sure enough, it was his new tooth, a handsome second bicuspid, which he would have the rest of his life.

Well, everything worked out just fine. Junior didn't have to take antibiotics and was spared nitrous oxide anesthesia by a specialist, and, of course, there was the saving of $500. Junior had just lost a baby tooth that was ready to fall out and allow the new tooth to come in. The baby tooth fragment moving around in the gum tissue caused the bleeding, and all that was needed was to have his dad there to take the tooth out with his fingers.

Henry Hackett's Story

Henry Hackett was a Navy veteran from the Korean War. He married Bertha just before he went overseas in 1952. They have three boys, two of whom are married, and four grandchildren. Henry had been a chief warrant officer on a destroyer tender. He lost most of his teeth in a fight in Sasebo, Japan, after a slight drunken misunderstanding at a Geisha bar. Henry forgot to duck when a sake bottle came flying across the room.

The shore patrol had to help Henry find his ship. At the time the tender was tied up with three destroyers that were taking on supplies while their crew members went ashore, stood watch, or spent time in the infirmary or dental clinic of the tender. Three dental officers were aboard ship. The second in command had the watch and took a look at Henry's smashed countenance.

The dentist, Lt. Frank Billiard, was a graduate of Baylor University Dental School with a doctorate in oral surgery. Henry was lucky because at first it looked as if he had a fractured cheek bone. At any rate, Henry had had many missing teeth already, and Lt. Billiard decided the rest would have to be extracted and replaced with full dentures.

Now, after fifty years and many sets of teeth, Henry's most recent upper denture had broken in half. Henry all through the years was always having problems with his dentures. Since he was a veteran, he could go to the Veteran's Administration and have his teeth replaced at little or no charge. But it's the same old story—you get what you pay for. Henry had received nothing but pain, floppy plates, and a chronic whistle when speaking.

Henry had signed up with a DHMO senior plan. And he thought that now was the time to use it. He had been assigned to a provider near his home, Dr. Lowell Ridge. He called the office and explained his problem. They would see him the next day. "Just drop in. We'll work you in," said Hilda, the office manager. In the meantime, Henry had repaired his broken denture with crazy glue.

Dr. Ridge's office was located in a small, single-story medical-dental building that housed five offices. There were three medical internists and two general dentists. Dr. Ridge was a recent graduate of the University of California at San Francisco Dental School. His was a single-dentist practice. He had two dental assistants, Hilda, and a hygienist, Pat.

Around 11:00 AM Henry parked his 1996 Honda in the handicapped parking area in front of the building. He had a permanent handicapped placard because of a back injury he had sustained about three years ago. He fell off the ladder while putting up a Santa Claus sleigh and reindeer display on his roof. It was an unfortunate accident because he had given up drinking after the Sasebo incident many years ago. There were no excuses.

The waiting room was void of patients. An artificial fichus plant stood in the corner, and an antiquated color TV that was tuned to reruns. There were ten rattan chairs and a magazine rack loaded with old issues of *Better Homes and Gardens* and *Road and Track*. He introduced himself to Hilda, who presented him with a clipboard loaded with the usual medical-dental history form, a consent form, and an arbitration form for his signature after she had made a copy of his DHMO card.

When Henry had completed his homework, he handed the board over to Hilda, who said, "Please take a seat for a few more minutes, and the doctor will see you." He was watching the last few minutes of the *Andy Griffith Show* when Hilda opened the door to the back office and asked Henry to please come on in.

Henry was seated in a slightly worn but comfortable dental chair. In walked Dr. Ridge, smiling and very relaxed. Henry felt the absence of anxiety. "Well, let's take a look at that plate," requested the good doctor. Henry took out his poorly repaired upper denture and handed it to the doctor. "Well, you split it right down the middle, Henry, and, I might say, you did a lousy repair job yourself," the doctor laughed. "I'll send this to the lab for a hot repair, which is much better than a cold cure type that is done in the office. Your plan does not cover lab repairs, but our fee is nominal, $125."

Ouch, thought Henry. "If that's the best for me, then go ahead."

"We'll get this back to you tomorrow morning. It's a little late now to get it back the same day," explained Dr. Ridge.

"That's okay, Doc. I brought one of my old uppers along with me just in case. What time tomorrow?"

"It'll be back by 10:00 AM at the latest," Dr. Ridge stated with a hint of 'I hope'." "You might be wise to call us at 9:30 just to be sure."

Henry left after giving Hilda a check. He was wearing his old upper plate against a non-matching lower. Hilda noticed Henry's little trick with the denture. She discreetly entered her observation in the patient's chart.

Hilda beat Henry to the punch the next morning. The lab had sent back the repaired denture early, so she called him at home and happily told him to get in as soon as possible.

Henry arrived at 9:45 for his teeth and was immediately shown into an operating room. Dr. Ridge was not there, but Hilda went into the back room and fetched his denture and returned to the seated Henry. "Here you are, Henry, all shiny and in one piece," she beamed. Henry took out his old upper plate and slipped in the repaired one. It felt weird and fat. He announced his immediate displeasure. Hilda reassured him, saying, "You put your old one in last night. After wearing the old one for around twelve hours, you get used to it, so the new one will feel odd for a short time."

Henry grudgingly accepted that explanation, thanked Hilda, and left.

Henry trudged into the front door of his house and plopped down in his favorite chair. He took out his upper denture and turned it over and around in his hands. "It's just too fat and rough," he groused to himself. He got up and went to his bedroom, opened his bureau drawer, pulled out a shoebox, and dumped about ten different dentures out on the bedspread. He studied each prosthetic, noting the many variations in thickness of each plate, color of the teeth, arrangement of the teeth, and the quality of the finish of each one. In his eyes they all looked better than his latest repaired denture.

Henry went back to his chair in the living room. His newly repaired denture hurt the roof of his mouth, and the edges of the plastic base cut his ridge.

Bertha arrived home from shopping. "Henry, would you help me with the groceries? There's about eight bags in the trunk." She hadn't noticed his funk. Henry shoved his teeth back into his mouth and stomped out to the garage. Once the groceries were put away, Henry explained his predicament. Bertha was sympathetic but urged Henry to remain calm. Her suggestion was simple: go back to the dentist and get a new set. Their DHMO plan covered denture replacements once the old dentures were at least five years old. There would be no charge unless Henry agreed to certain upgrades.

So the next morning, Henry called the dentist for an appointment. Hilda wisely refrained from asking questions and made him an appointment for 10:00 AM in one week. After much huffing and puffing on his part, Henry acquiesced to the time. A week of torture seemed to be unavoidable. He was advised to leave his dentures out for at least twenty-four hours before the appointment. This would ensure that his oral tissues would not be inflamed or flattened from the pressures of the old dentures.

Henry ate soup for the twenty-four hours before his appointment with Dr. Ridge. The doctor was on time, and he greeted Henry with a smile and a handshake. "How are you getting along?" asked Dr. Ridge He immediately realized that he had asked a question that would receive a negative response.

A litany of profane complaints followed. Then came the next mistake. Dr. Ridge held the upper denture, felt the plastic edges, and scrutinized the plastic teeth. "Henry, it looks like you've been working on these flanges with a nail file and some sandpaper," he commented. That comment had to go down in history as number one on the stupid list.

There was a real chance for continued problems due to two factors: an irritable, non-compliant patient and a fairly young dentist who had little training in fabricating full dentures and probably should have referred the patient to a specialist in dentures (prosthodontist). The second issue was a two-way street because the patient didn't want to spend extra money and insisted that Dr. Ridge do the procedure.

Another problem was that Henry had very little supporting bone left. Even though he was an experienced denture patient, the chances for a perfect result were remote.

In spite of all the negatives, Dr. Ridge dived into the case. He managed to get an extra $500 (in addition to the original $150) for the use of porcelain teeth and special staining of the denture bases.

It took seven appointments for Dr. Ridge to complete the case. This is the appropriate standard of treatment for full upper and lower dentures and suggests that he used the best possible technique to achieve a satisfactory result. Every appointment was a test of Dr. Ridge's patience and stamina because of the crotchety Henry. He was continually challenging the hard-working dentist's technique, mainly because he had never received such treatment. The bombardment of inane questions was almost more than any sane man could withstand.

Upon delivery of the dentures, Dr. Ridge was proud of his work. They looked great, and the bite was textbook. He even got a smile from Henry, who checked the dentist's workmanship in a handheld mirror.

This story has a happy ending. After a few bite adjustments, Henry seemed to manage quite well. The moral here is that the construction of full upper and lower dentures is a team endeavor. It demands great perseverance on the part of the dentist and the unconditional cooperation from the patient.

Henry never switched dentures again. He put his files and sandpaper away.

Full dentures are being replaced by various types of implants and have become highly successful. However, they are not a covered benefit in most plans and are very expensive. It is likely that they will become a benefit in the near future as the DHMOs compete for patients, but dentists should know how to make full dentures when they are the only option.

Can't I just get my teeth cleaned?

Hugh had perfect teeth. He was in his sixties and had never had a cavity. His impacted wisdom teeth were extracted when he was sixteen. When Hugh was a youth, the family dentist, Dr. Walter Symington, was located in downtown Los Angeles. He was on the seventh floor of a tall building that was home to attorneys, physicians, jewelers, and other sophisticated businesses. The building had been built in 1932 and was nothing but class, lots of gold gilt, ornate facades, marble floors, and elevators with neatly uniformed elevator boys and an elevator manager who held a hand clicker to signal availability. His uniform mimicked an admiral.

Hugh's mother faithfully had sent her son to the dentist every six months without fail. Now sixty-eight, Hugh still had twenty-eight perfect teeth. He had married his high school sweetheart, Kay, forty-five years ago. They had three sons, who for many years were patients of Dr. Symington along with their mother. The entire family, which included three daughters-in law and seven grandchildren, had managed to have little or no problems with their teeth. They all loved Dr. Symington. He had taken care of all of them, even when the kids were little. And he had managed to treat the young ones without knocking them out. The toy box was the negotiating factor that resulted in happy dental experiences.

Dr. Symington was long gone, but Hugh and his family had stayed with the practice, and he had maintained his six-month recall cleaning visits through the years. However, in recent years Dr. Ahmad Aziz, Symington's successor, had become a provider for several of the DHMOs in addition to maintaining his private practice. Hugh's employer had contracted with a DHMO, and Dr. Aziz was on its panel.

Now Hugh's cleanings were a covered benefit at no charge. It seemed strange to Hugh at the time, but his relationship with Dr. Aziz became a little different. It no longer gave him a feeling of comfort and friendship. When Hugh would go in for his cleaning, he was bombarded with the latest in treatments of gum disease, many of which were not covered benefits. Because they were not covered, the dentist could charge his usual and customary fees. They would now chart his periodontal pockets and explain the need for special gum treatments, such as irrigation and administration of local antibiotics to ensure perfect gum health.

Beatrice, the office manager, would patiently explain to Hugh the rationale for these expensive treatments. "But," Hugh asked almost tearfully, "can't I just get my teeth cleaned like I always did before?"

"Oh my, no," answered Beatrice. "Dr. Aziz is now using the latest techniques, which will literally guarantee dental health for the rest of your life. But you must be sure to get in every six months like before to maintain the optimum."

"You mean it's going to cost me $250 every time I get my teeth cleaned?" asked Hugh. "Before I got these 'benefits' I never paid more than $25, and my teeth have always been perfect. Actually, before my insurance I was much more comfortable with the treatment. I could sit up in the chair, the dentist would squirt water in my mouth every so often, I would spit out in the cuspidor, and it took about forty minutes. Now the new equipment means they lay me back, put an uncomfortable plastic suction in my mouth that usually hurts, and tell me I can't spit. There's no cuspidor. It's more expensive and more uncomfortable, and it takes fifteen minutes. And I never see the doctor until the staff has x-rayed and charted me. I think he should see me first and then decide what x-rays are needed, like before."

"Well, if you're not happy with our service, it might be best for you to go elsewhere for your dental maintenance," Beatrice replied sarcastically.

"That's a good idea," Hugh said. "I'm going to call my carrier and ask to be moved, hopefully to a non-thief type. Maybe I'll get my teeth cleaned the old-fashioned way. I'm going to cancel my dental plan with your office. I know my children have not been happy because they are always sent out to a specialist. The personal touch has been missing anyway. No more toy box. Maybe we all can find an old-fashioned dentist."

It took a long time, but Hugh's persistence finally paid off. After enrolling and dis-enrolling three more dentists, he finally realized the only chance he had was to find a single practitioner who was a little older and not in a large medical-dental facility. He found Dr. Xavier Saviers, who occupied a one-story, six-office building. Dr. Saviers owned the building, which housed a chiropractor, two real estate agents, two attorneys, and a tarot card reader.

It was perfect. Dr. Saviers's office had cuspidors. Hugh could see "no thief" all over the place. Dr. Saviers had a receptionist, Evelyn, and a chair-side assistant, June. No clipboards, no hustle. Dr. Saviers examined each patient *before* deciding which x-rays were needed. He examined Hugh's mouth, smiled, and said, "Wow, what beautiful teeth! You obviously have been taking excellent care of them. You have very little plaque, just some tartar around the lower front teeth and the upper molars in the back where the saliva gland dumps concentrated, salty saliva when stimulated."

Dr. Saviers scaled the tartar off his teeth and then polished them with a rubber cup and pumice, using a high-torque polishing handpiece. He was then given a cup of mint mouth rinse to swish and expectorate into the handy cuspidor.

Hugh got up from the chair, thanked Dr. Saviers, stopped by the front desk, paid his co-payment, made a six-month recall appointment, and left with a comfortable aftertaste.

Hugh saw *one dentist*. The key to a happy patient is the one-on-one relationship with the doctor. Today, it's a real problem for the patient when he sees more than one dentist for treatment. There is a definite breakdown in the time-honored doctor-patient relationship. There also is a breakdown in the continuity of care. Each dentist has his own way of doing things. Bouncing from doctor to doctor just doesn't result in consistent care and follow-up. Each dentist will always find something wrong with the previous guy's work, which confuses the patient. It is incumbent on the patient to always ask questions and make a deliberate decision based on a careful analysis of the proposed treatment plan. The patient must not sign on the dotted at the initial visit because of the selling pressure, and should go home and think about it first. Unless there is a toothache, no immediate treatment is needed.

Please note that it is below the standard of dental care for a patient to be x-rayed before seeing the dentist. It is the dentist's responsibility to decide which x-rays should be taken, not the dental assistant's. This has become common practice in most dental offices, and is blatantly wrong.

Chapter 27

True Personal Stories

Gloria's Story

Gloria, my fantastic wife of many years, made a dental appointment with one of the providers who were contracted with my company. In fact, I had audited this office many times and found Dr. Gladiola You to be a fine dentist, whose facility and charts passed with flying colors. Glad, as we knew her, had a very busy practice with several dentists who acted as hygienists. Gloria made her initial appointment to have her teeth x-rayed and cleaned.

Since this was her initial appointment, she received a clipboard with a myriad of forms to be completed. Once she completed these forms, Gloria paid her $20 co-payment and was seated first in the x-ray room (digital images), and then was escorted to the dental operating room. She never saw Glad. In popped an associate dentist, Dr. Huang Tran. She went through Gloria's mouth with a mirror and a periodontal probe, which measures the depth of the little troughs around the teeth and always makes the patient feel that something important is happening because it hurts. These depths were charted on a sophisticated form showing all the surfaces of the teeth. Dr. Tran probed around her mouth, tsking and sighing, tsking and sighing, tsking and sighing.

In an uncomfortable panic, Gloria asked, "What's wrong? Are my teeth that bad?"

"Well," said the doctor solemnly, "you have many gum-line cavities that need immediate restoration, and you have three fillings that need replacing, and a new crown replacing an old gold crown on your lower left side." "I'll finish cleaning your teeth today, but you must make an appointment as soon as possible for Dr. You, who is your assigned dentist, to restore your mouth to appropriate dental health."

"Dr. You hasn't even looked at my mouth. Shouldn't she examine me now to verify your diagnosis?" asked an incredulous Gloria.

"Oh, no," answered the self-assured dentist, "Dr. You relies heavily on me, and, of course, she'll re-evaluate my diagnosis when she sees you."

Then Gloria sarcastically asked, "May I have the x-rays? I would like my husband to look them over before I agree to your treatment plan."

"Well," Tran shrieked, "what would he know? It's just a waste of time."

"Well," answered Gloria aping the dentist's arrogance, "my husband happens to be a dentist, and has audited this office many times, giving it high grades—of course, before you were here."

Said the flabbergasted Huang, "Maybe this treatment can be placed on hold until your next examination appointment."

"For your information, Dr. Pedersen has been aware of some of the problems you mentioned, and those so-called defective fillings and the crown have been there for forty years. Please don't insult our intelligence," commented my agitated spouse. "I know that he'll contact Dr. You when he audits the office in the near future and probably will discuss my dental condition at that time. You might even be still working here! Of course, I know that you're probably under the gun to drum up new business, especially procedures that are not covered benefits to generate profits."

"Another thing," Gloria continued, "my husband knows those gum-line cavities have been there for years. He has said that composite restorations in those areas of my teeth would give me nothing but toothaches or sensitivity because of the chemicals that are required to bond the material to the dentine of the tooth. And my teeth have always been very sensitive to cold, even before the crown, which is still in perfect shape."

The eager dentist was de-tsked, and Gloria was given a six-month recall appointment. It was a narrow escape.

The Dingbat

I have perfect teeth—no cavities and no periodontal disease. So when I go to the dentist, I go there to get my teeth cleaned, and that's it. I do have a filling. I had it done when I was in dental school, young, adventurous, and stupid. I had a classmate drill a hole in my upper left first molar without anesthetic to see how it felt. *It hurt like hell!* In those years, all we had were handpieces that could muster up 3,500 RPM with steel drills. (The new drills go 500,000 RPM with carbide burs.) The noise and the stink along with the pain gave me understanding and compassion for the dental patient when working on him. As a result, I turned out to be a gentle dentist, I hope. At least nobody complained, and they kept coming back.

I went to Dr. Gladiola You, the dentist I recommended for my wife. In spite of Gloria's troubles with the office, I figured that since Dr. You knew me she would give me preferential treatment—meaning, just cleaning my teeth and letting me go. I was wrong.

Dr. You had made enough loot to buy an entire building across the street from her old office. This attests to the financial success of her practice, which Gloria narrowly escaped from being a heavy financial contributor. So my appointment was at her new streamlined office in the new building.

In spite of the fact the office was almost completely computerized and paperless, I still had to fill out all the forms and disclaimers except for the ones that were set up on those touch screens. When you sign them, your signature looks like you had a stroke. Dr. You's office is a magnificent place, with high ceilings, crown molding, piped-in music, brand new equipment, and an elaborate aquarium in the waiting room with all kinds of exotic fish flitting through the tank. It tends to hypnotize and quiet the antsy patient and helps pass the long waiting times.

After my thirty-minute wait, I was ushered into the x-ray room even after I had said I didn't want x-rays. The x-ray room was equipped with a dental chair and a digital x-ray head mounted on the chair. I sat there listening to the music and waiting. After a half-hour, in walked a young dental assistant wearing a green dental gown. "Who are you?" I asked.

"Well, sir, I'm the boyfriend of Dr. You's daughter," he answered with a smile.

"How long have you been a dental assistant?"

"About three weeks," he replied. "Dr. You's daughter has been teaching me."

I continued my questions. "Have you been accredited?"

"I don't think so."

"How many x-rays have you taken?"

"You're my second patient."

"Why are you in here?"

"To take x-rays of your mouth."

"You only have to take bitewings then."

"What are bitewings?"

I now knew I was being x-rayed by a dingbat. With great patience, I showed him how to take bitewings using the digital x-ray head. My first, second, and third impressions of this kid were the same. He, indeed, was a dingbat. After that half-hour session with the amateur assistant, I was moved to another elegant operating room with the high ceiling, crown molding, and serene, piped-in music. Another half-hour wait. Then in came a tiny dentist named Hong Nguyen, who looked about twelve. Luckily, she was not the dentist who had seen Gloria.

Actually, this wisp of a woman did a pretty fair job of scaling my teeth without the usual diatribe about brushing, massaging gums, and diet. We talked mostly about where she went to dental school and when she graduated, which was last year. Swell. Everybody was an amateur in this office except Dr. You.

Then she said that she was through with her part and that the dental assistant would polish my teeth to complete the cleaning.

In walked Dingbat! I was his second patient; so I received a polished nose, cheek, and lips. After being slopped all over by this joker, I leaped out of the chair yelling, "Enough already!" Dingbat stood there nonplussed and tried to reassure me. I said, "Are you kidding?" I left the room and went to the front desk, with its high-polished marble top, and asked to see Dr. You.

Dr. You came from the back and greeted me with a fond smile, which turned to a frown. I advised her in no uncertain terms that it was against the law (California Dental Practice Act) to employ unlicensed people to perform dental procedures. I told her that it is too bad that her beautiful office had declined in status to becoming a money machine instead of a professional office like it used to be.

Dingbat is history. I have subsequently changed dentists. I found a dentist and hygienist closer to home who are skillful and honest. They are unique in today's world of greed and low morality. Confidentially, I went there before Gloria had her first appointment and forewarned about up-selling. So far it has worked out, and we're both happy with them.

Patients should always check the credentials of the dentist and staff before accepting treatment. Every facility should have a list of the staff, including assistants, placed in a conspicuous site for easy viewing. Dr. You's office did have the appropriate display, which unfortunately did not list Dingbat.

Chapter 28

Evidence-based Dentistry

Life has been made easier for the dentist with the advent of new materials and new dental devices. However, the costs of running a dental practice have become astronomic. Thus, there is always pressure to produce. Unfortunately, such pressure has compelled many practitioners to become creative in their treatment planning for the trusting patient. The preceding fictional situations, except for Gloria's and mine, give you an idea of just how important it is to find a dentist you can trust.

The replacement of the old-fashioned single dental practice by a large, multifaceted practice has some benefits, such as having all the specialties under one roof. But the large practice loses the personal touch that existed with the single doctor and the two-chair office. Also, continuity of care suffers. By "continuity of care" I mean that when the dentist and the patient arrive at an appropriate treatment plan, the dentist performs all the stages of the treatment in a logical sequence until completion. For example, the condition of the gum tissues must be fixed before doing any restorative work. If the dentist made a crown on a tooth before cleaning up the gums, the gums would likely shrink and expose the edges of the crown. I'll bet you have friends who have crowns on their front teeth that have black lines around them. That's because the crowns were made *before* fixing the gums. This indicates that there was an illogical sequence of procedures in the treatment plan.

Evidence-based dentistry has been discussed in the dental literature for many years. All it means is that the treatment planned for the patient is based entirely on the actual dental needs of the patient. Evidence-based ideas stress the importance of a concise, accurate appraisal of the needs of the patient and the means of restoration that makes sense, with a minimum of extras. There is also an implication that the patient is restricted from self-diagnosis, which is tantamount to telling the dentist how to practice.

Moral for the dentist: Many dentists succumb to the dictatorial patient. Such benign behavior of the dentist usually results in poor dental outcomes. Please, Doctors, be thorough in your analyses of the patient's needs. Create diagnoses and treatment plans that make sense, and be firm when patients try to dictate treatment. Moreover, please never allow the possibility of unneeded upgrades to sway your judgment.

Moral for patients: Always be accurate with your chief complaint. Listen to the diagnosis. Bide your time in making a decision. Have confidence in your doctor, and then be a compliant patient. This means following all the post-operative instructions, recommendations, and keeping recall appointments. And don't forget that the treatment should be done in a logical sequence. When in doubt, *ask!*

In defense of the dentist: Many treatment plans give the appearance of price gouging. However, they are created because dentists fear plaintiff attorneys and frivolous lawsuits. Remember, my last patient was a seven-year old boy, who stated, "If you hurt me, I'll sue you!" Unfortunately, it's the sign of the times.

Afterword

I am still in the DHMO business working part-time as a dental consultant. Still handling grievances. Still working Quality Management. Still talking dentistry. I love it!

The professional and ethical status of dentistry is under attack by practitioners who have lost their way. The twenty-first century way of life in our country has changed. The trend toward greed as being life's motivator is leading new generations into a morass of immorality. It's scary!

It would be fantastic to have the dental profession become a profession again instead of a business. It would be fantastic for a patient to go to the dentist and receive evidence-based treatment. It would be fantastic for the patient to go to the dentist and leave without a huge, unanticipated financial obligation.

It's not an impossible dream!

Dr. P.

Printed in the United States
by Baker & Taylor Publisher Services